DiAnne,

Thank you for your graciousness and selflessness as you helped me to " find the runway and land the plane." I remain forever grateful.

Janet

AKA
MHH

Forever Yankee

A Love Song for My Family

Mary Howland Harrington

This book is a work of non-fiction. Unless otherwise noted, the author
and the publisher make no explicit guarantees as to the accuracy of
the information contained in this book and in some cases, names of
people and places have been altered to protect their privacy.

LifeRich Publishing is a registered trademark of
The Reader's Digest Association, Inc.

LifeRich Publishing books may be ordered through booksellers or by contacting:

LifeRich Publishing
1663 Liberty Drive
Bloomington, IN 47403
www.liferichpublishing.com
1 (888) 238-8637

Because of the dynamic nature of the Internet, any web addresses or
links contained in this book may have changed since publication and
may no longer be valid. The views expressed in this work are solely those
of the author and do not necessarily reflect the views of the publisher,
and the publisher hereby disclaims any responsibility for them.

Any people depicted in stock imagery provided by Thinkstock are models,
and such images are being used for illustrative purposes only.
Certain stock imagery © Thinkstock.

ISBN: 978-1-4897-1026-0 (sc)
ISBN: 978-1-4897-1025-3 (e)

Library of Congress Control Number: 2016917729

Print information available on the last page.

LifeRich Publishing rev. date: 01/19/2017

To my Forever Marine, and the love of my life
Semper Fi

Table of Contents

Acknowledgments

The idea of writing this book percolated in my mind for three decades before I was able to commit the time required to begin the project. My parents, Mary and Thurston, had sold the family home in Claypool and relocated to Florida to escape the harsh northern Ohio winters. As they downsized their belongings prior to their departure, each of us kids was encouraged to lay claim to certain treasures that could or should not be moved. Among the items I chose were the family photographs and slides of our family vacations that were carefully catalogued by my mother. I also selected my mother's journals of those same trips. From these and the collected memories of all my siblings this project emerged.

I cannot begin to express my thanks to all those who assisted me in this endeavor. However, I would like to extend a special "shout-out" to those people who spent not a little time or effort helping me to hone my craft and to complete this project.

First and foremost is my husband whose love, patience, loyalty and superb listening skills coached me through the process. He is truly a rare gem.

Appropriately, the next person I must mention is Amanda Chandler, my third grade teacher. She was the first person in my life who invited me to keep developing my imagination and to record my observations and feelings. She is gone now, and I only regret that she didn't live to receive my thanks or read this book. Others followed: James Baldwin, another teacher who, while I was in high school, devoted his Saturday mornings to teach a small group of us who loved writing and who were passionate about learning as much as we could about the writing process prior to entering college. And finally my good teacher, colleague, and friend, Kevin Hoskinson, who encouraged me to develop this book. His periodic nudging me to completion was incredibly timely and helped me through more than one case of writer's block. Without him this book would not have been finished.

DiAnne Schmidt, you are the best and most thorough of editors and a very special friend. I appreciate your comments, your meticulous work as you helped me polish the manuscript, and especially your wonderful sense of humor as we worked, sang, learned, and worshipped together.

Lastly, the entire Liferich team helped make publishing this memoir smooth and painless. So Wendy Morris and Adam Tinsley, and all the design team…thank you.

MHH

Introduction

Situated on the east side of the Connecticut River in the Pioneer Valley, the city of Summerfield was one of the most vibrant cities in New England. This community's mid-1950s, post-World War II population represented every country in Europe and some regions of Africa and Asia. The premier medical center, the schools, the libraries, the colleges, the universities, the access to the Berkshire Hills to the west, and the public green spaces where families could enjoy vigorous outdoor activities defined Summerfield as the "City Beautiful" and the "Gateway to the Berkshires."

Like the rest of the city, our densely populated neighborhood teemed with a multitude of characters of varying backgrounds and multiple languages. This endless array of people, cultures, and languages enriched my early childhood and fostered an unquenchable curiosity about people and geography that continues to this day.

Although our nuclear family consisted of two parents and the five of us children, our numbers were frequently enlarged by an extended family of grandparents, aunts, uncles, and cousins too numerous to count. We crossed multiple generations and numerous religious denominations; our interests spread from stamp collecting and golf to history, music, technology, and literature. This diversity, which continues today, sharpened our intellects and fostered tolerance toward other people that no formal education could possible achieve. Our parents' immediate descendants include tree surgeons, communications experts, engineers, teachers, musicians, administrative assistants, systems analysts, building managers, a budding political scientist, and representatives from every branch of military service.

The unifying threads in this colorful milieu were our birthright as New Englanders and the constant presence of our parents – parents who were too old by a decade to be considered part of the Greatest Generation but were too young to be included in the Lost Generation. Our mother was a woman with the narrow upbringing and the rigid conscience typical for a woman born in 1911 to a first generation Scotsman and a second generation Canadian. She was undisputedly the manager of all things domestic in our household while Dad was the breadwinner. At the time he and Mother moved to Summerfield a few years prior to Marilyn's birth in 1943, Dad was supporting a wife, three children, and providing regular financial assistance to his own parents. Additionally, he was providing help to his parents-in-law. He had recently been hired by Pratt and Whitney – a most fortunate occurrence from the family's standpoint. Working on aircraft engines in a protected industry allowed him to contribute to the World War II home front efforts and continue to support his every-growing family without an extended overseas absence.

Outwardly we appeared to be a normal family. However, discerning observers would note that Mother had distinct artistic tendencies. She was nervous, sensitive, quick tempered, impatient, and often frustrated by the narrow confines of her life as a wife, household manager, and parent. She loved music, literature, and history passionately, and she was happiest when she was travelling to new destinations and meeting new and interesting people. Plagued by what was probably attention deficit disorder her entire life, Mother was a compulsive talker, organizer, and planner. Compensating for what I think she recognized but never openly acknowledged as a serious disability, she functioned through the use of a rigid routine and daily lists and was easily thrown into total disarray by any interruptions or deviations from her routine or lists. With five kids and a huge extended family, interruptions were all too common, and Mother tended to be in a constant state of turmoil.

Dad was usually the anchor of our often-stormy household. While the escapades of us five kids often drove our mother to intense anger or hysteria, most of the time Dad adopted a kids-will-be-kids attitude. When we kids came home muddied and bruised, Mother was angry and impatient whereas Dad remained patient and calm and more often than not would patch us up. While Mother always became upset by any detours or derailments in her routine, Dad would relax into a spirit of adventure. He never expected life to be smooth and ordered, and, I suspect, he preferred it not to be. Dad was a socially skilled introvert, comfortable in his own skin, highly sensitive and self-aware. He once told me that had the circumstances of his life allowed, he would have liked to have been a teacher or perhaps a counselor. Dad was intrigued by technology, loved learning, and was years ahead of his own generation in his passion for environmental issues. Like Mother, Dad had a great wanderlust: he loved to travel.

In spite of their differences, Mother and Dad were deeply in love all of their married life. When I was younger, I thought that their marriage was based on a complete and mutual misunderstanding of one another. While this may have been true sometimes, they shared many traits.

The first trait they shared was frugality. This was evident from the start. They didn't have money to pay for a wedding, so they were married in a church parlor on the third of July in 1932. They were married on a weekend so Dad wouldn't have to take any time off from work. (That New-England/Puritan work ethic wouldn't allow that.) Even if they had had the money, they wouldn't have had a church wedding. Church weddings were expensive. That didn't fit in with frugality.

They shared a love for the simple pleasures in life. For Mother and Dad a day at the harbor in New Bedford watching ships come in and out of the docks was as much fun as going to the theatre and required much less dressing up. Carrying a picnic lunch and riding a street car to the beach for an afternoon in the sun and surf was another simple pleasure they enjoyed. And they never missed a chance to attend a dance in the New Bedford armory: a fun, inexpensive treat.

Another value they shared was that of voting. Voting their conscience (Mother's conscience usually lined up with Dad's in this instance) was as important as Sunday dinner with one set of grandparents or another. Participating in the democratic processes of community, state, and nation was a privilege and responsibility that Dad impressed – with great emphasis – upon all of his children. He never missed voting in an election until he became too sick to cast a rational vote. Everything about my parents made them quintessential New Englanders.

But New Englanders they were not allowed to remain. 1956 was a watershed year for the entire family. That year Dad and Mother moved to Ohio with Marilyn, Sam the dog, and me in tow; both our nuclear family and our extended family were fractured. We left behind a beautiful, vibrant, cosmopolitan city to move to a small community that consisted of one very crowded school housing thirteen grades, a volunteer fire department, a mom-and-pop general store, one bank, two protestant churches, and two housing developments – or allotments as they were referred to. The rest of the community – called a township – consisted of farms, with dairy operations predominating. The non-farmers in Claypool mostly worked either at one of the local mills that processed iron or at the wire harness plant affiliated with a car manufacturing company.

Dad was neither a farmer nor did he work manufacturing steel or wire harnesses. He was a metallurgist employed as a quality control manager. Although he was "stationed" at a plant near Claypool, he was still accountable to his supervisors in Connecticut. When we moved into our small ranch house, most of our neighbors thought Dad's work-place arrangements were a little odd if not downright threatening.

Our family was considered different not only by virtue of Dad's employment, but also by the fact that we were clearly from the East (evident by our strong Berkshire accents). At times we spoke a different language, and had different values. These oddities stood out in a small township where everyone was closely related and where the community's mores were narrow and strictly adhered to. Culture shock was inevitable for all of us!

As the following stories unfold, they take us – the family and the reader – from Massachusetts to Ohio and far beyond the first years of initial acclimatization. And even though after a time we adopted many Midwestern characteristics, we remained firmly rooted in Yankeedom because of Mother's insistence that we learn as much as possible about our cultural heritage, and because of Dad's willingness to spent part of almost every summer he could driving to New England to reconnect with the rest of our family.

For Marilyn and me, growing up with one foot in each culture was extremely difficult. Now, however, I am grateful for the experience, for not only did she and I become much closer than I think we might have if we'd stayed in Summerfield, but we also learned that home was not so much a physical dwelling place as it was something that will always live in our hearts.

We are like Mother and Dad – and Grace, Bradford, and Adela – forever Yankees.

Chapter 1

BLAST OFF

The concrete sidewalks steamed. Following an unusually hot and muggy week, a late-day thunderstorm had crossed the Connecticut River that Saturday and dropped a welcome, cooling rain over the city of Summerfield. In its aftermath the air smelled of ozone and wet pavement. The grass gleamed emerald. Mother hated loud noises and was absolutely terrified of anything that produced electricity. She had shooed her entire flock of kids into the house at the first clap of thunder. There we were forced to remain in sweating discomfort until we were given the all clear. Released from the torrid prison of the kitchen at the storm's end, all five of us kids gathered on the front porch.

Grace, the oldest, was characteristically engaged in filing and polishing her nails. She was nineteen and had started working at a local Lerner's shop selling women's clothing. Bradford, second in line, had returned home after a hard day of work at Joey's Drug Store. At seventeen and a half years old he was filled with dreams and ambition and was saving his money for college. Not just any college either. After graduating from high school Bradford had set his heart on Babson College in Wellesley where he planned to join his good friend Angus McLean. Adela was reading a book and smiling over some happy thought related to her church youth group. Like Bradford and Grace with their jobs, Adela, third in line, had found her own Mother- approved venue for staying away from home as much as possible. She had already invested a considerable amount of her time and energy with her youth group and looked forward to tomorrow's meeting with joyful anticipation.

Marilyn, the one who came before me, had put away her key skates when the storm moved in. How I envied her those skates! Bright chrome with an adjustable length and width, these skates could be strapped onto Marilyn's shoes and the toe clamps tightened with a special key. The key hung from a lanyard looped around her neck. Marilyn raced around the neighborhood on those skates, starting from the front of our house and heading north on David Road, then turning west onto Black Street, making a silky left turn onto Leominster Terrace and finally gliding up to Cameron Street where she would turn smoothly around and skate the reverse trip home. I loved the sound of those skates on the sidewalks! I couldn't wait until I was old enough to have my own pair, but at four I was small for my age, and the tightest setting on a pair of key skates was too big for my feet. Dad told me that I would have to wait at least a year before Mother could find a pair of skates that would fit me.

He and Mother soon joined us on the porch. A northerner by both birth and genetics, Mother never fared well during heat waves. Though none of us knew it then, Mother had suffered with asthma since childhood and also had serious allergies. Coughing, wheezing, sneezing and headaching her way through many humid summers in the Pioneer Valley, Mother was her own worst enemy. Her physical problems were aggravated by her refusal to use any type of window or ceiling fan–she said they were too extravagant, and we had to economize because Bradford and Adela were preparing for college. My own perception was that Mother's concerns were less about the fans costing too much to operate and more about the fact that they ran on electricity. In Mother's mind, anything electrical was highly dangerous, and a house that used too much electricity was likely to erupt in sparks, flames, or explosions.

Mother's fears of such fires were not totally unfounded. The two circuits of nob and tube wire installed much earlier in the century were barely adequate to support even the kitchen of our modest home. Dad's full-time occupation on the weekend was replacing fuses on the kitchen circuit; this kept Mother happy and free from excess electricity induced anxiety.

Because she had spent most of the day in the kitchen doing laundry with the old wringer washer (blowing two fuses in the process), cooking meals, and keeping track of Marilyn and me in the unforgiving heat Mother was spent, both physically and mentally. She had caught up a magazine when she retired to the porch and sat down in a wicker chair positioned so as to catch every breeze floating across the city.

Dad himself was tired with good reason. After commuting to and from Connecticut all week, he had been up early on this particular Saturday with a laborious task facing him. He decided to process and cap several gallons of his famous, special, root beer for the family's enjoyment.

With one income supporting five kids, two adults, and two grandparents, store-bought soda was beyond our family's means. But Dad's homemade root beer surpassed anything available in any store in the East as far as we were concerned, and we were delighted to have it. Carefully rationed and judiciously shared with family members and special friends, two bottlings could last us several months.

Spurred on by our lavish praise and pride in his domestic accomplishment, Dad sweltered his way through the many bottles, mixing and capping, and then carefully stacking case upon case of newly processed soft drinks in the cellar. Marilyn and I were forbidden to intrude on this process, and the older kids were busy with their various pursuits. Other than the occasional diversion of changing fuses so Mother could finish the laundry, Dad was left to peacefully and methodically go about his work. He emerged from the cellar late in the day drenched with perspiration and happily gratified about his contribution to the family's well-being. He pulled up a chair on the porch, picked up his newspaper, and sat down next to Mother.

Dad was no more than cooling off when Mother thinned her lips in the unique way of well-bred New England women of that generation.

"Will you look at that!" she muttered.

"Look at what?" murmured Dad. He was deep into his paper.

"Why, Vince Cavelli just stepped onto his porch wearing nothing but boxer shorts and an undershirt!" Mother was properly scandalized. "And he's drinking beer from a bottle!!"

At her pronouncement the rest of us looked up as well. Sure enough, Mr. Cavelli was sitting on his porch clothed in his underwear and enjoying a well-deserved beer.

I didn't understand why Mr. Cavelli sitting on his porch in his underwear on a hot August night and enjoying a cold beer was so awful, but in Mother's curiously constructed mind only an occasional sip of wine or a mixed drink was allowable (provided the person consuming it was using the correct glass). Drinking beer was, in her opinion, coarse and vulgar. Quaffing beer straight from the bottle was beyond her vocabulary to describe. I was honestly confused, although I had learned very early not to question Mother's values in this or in any other regard. Mother's responses were not always versed in logic; she did not seem to have any need to change. Her own thinking, however flawed, suited her just fine. Gentlemen did not appear on their front porches in boxer shorts and "grandpa" undershirts or drink beer from a bottle at any time. That was that.

In Mother's opinion the only thing more objectionable than Mr. Cavelli's underwear and beer was Mr. Erickson's cigars. Mother was of the opinion that smoking was a terrible character deficiency and that Mr. Erickson smoked far too many stogies for a neighbor who lived next door to us. Apparently Mrs. Erickson shared Mother's sentiments regarding the stogies. Unless the temperature was below zero, Mr. Erickson was sent outside to smoke. Consequently, during the summer months, Mother was constantly assailed by the smoke from cheap cigars wafting into the kitchen and further aggravating her allergies.

While Mother fumed not quite sotto voce about the neighbors' assaults on her sensibilities, the rest of us attempted to return to our activities.

"I'm really thirsty. I want some root-beer," I begged Dad.

"The lady-like way to ask is to say 'please' and the correct verb is 'may,'" Dad responded.

He was always irritated by bad manners, incorrect grammar, and sloppy diction. Poor enunciation and the use of slang resulted in an immediate reminder of proper word usage.

"Besides," he continued, "we have to wait for the root beer to mature."

"How long will that be?" I asked.

"A while. If you're thirsty go get some water."

Dad's response was meant to put my begging to rest for a while.

My four year old mind didn't grasp the concept of later. Within fifteen minutes I repeated my request.

"Please, may I have some root-beer now?"

"No. You have to be very patient with home-made tonic. It takes a long time to mature.

It will probably be ready in a month or so," Dad explained.

A few moments later a series of loud bangs followed by the sound of breaking glass broke everyone's concentration again.

Dad looked up quickly, but not as quickly as Mother.

"Someone's shooting at our windows!" she shrieked.

At this wild pronouncement, Grace carefully capped her nail polish, Bradford quickly rose from his chair, and Adela laid down the book she had been reading and glanced up at Bradford and Grace with a resigned sigh. The first thunderstorm of the day had passed by, but a second storm of greater ferocity was brewing on our front porch and Grace, Bradford and Adela knew it.

Both the sound and frequency of the noise escalated quickly into a series of ear-splitting explosions.

The sound was very close to the porch.

At this moment the rest of us recognized what the three older kids already had discovered. The sound was coming not from outside our house, but from within. A cacophony of noise and shattering glass suggested that someone was setting off a large volume of firecrackers in our cellar.

"Fire!" Mother screamed. "Fire! The house is on fire! I knew that thunderstorm caused a problem when the lights flickered! Call the fire department! Call the police!"

With another outburst she rushed into the living room to snatch what valuables she could before the flames consumed the house.

Marilyn, meanwhile, knew what to do in case of fire. At Mother's first shrieks of fire, she grabbed me firmly by the hand and rushed me out to the sidewalk in front of the house. As we stood there waiting for the fire department and the police to arrive, the rest of the drama quickly unfolded.

The frenzy on our front porch aroused Mr. Cavelli, Mr. Erickson who had just started another cigar in his front yard, and the Winthrop family on the other side of our house. They had rushed to the scene at the first indication of fire, Mr. Cavelli still in his underwear and Mr. Erickson with his cigar clenched between his teeth, to find Mother in full vibrato, Grace clutching her nail polish, and Marilyn and me standing on the front sidewalk bewildered and waiting for the public authorities to rescue us. Adela and Bradford had gone to look for Dad who had quietly disappeared down the cellar stairs. Bradford found him there, standing in abject misery amid a small mountain of shattered glass with several gallons of root beer flowing freely around his feet.

"The root-beer exploded," reported Bradford to Mother. "Everything is okay, but the cellar is a mess."

Indeed, a combination of excessive heat, the placement of the cases of root-beer near a sunny cellar window, and an over-abundance of the carbonating yeast had caused a chain reaction. Every bottle of tonic that Dad had so carefully processed had exploded violently. The cellar was a sticky mess of root beer, broken glass, and flooded coal bin.

When Mother ventured into the cellar, her reaction was predictable.

She went berserk with anger and righteous indignation. Her peace had been challenged beyond all reason. She'd had a hot and miserable day in the kitchen. She had been looking forward to a quiet evening on her front porch and had been assaulted by violent explosions, neighbors racing into her space wearing nothing but their underwear or smoking cheap cigars, a nine year old refusing to go into the house, a frightened preschooler still standing on the sidewalk looking orphaned and unnerved, three teenagers trying to stifle their giggles, and a debris-filled basement.

Dad was a mixture of emotions. Wanting a little peace and quiet himself, he also was aware that on this occasion he had been the sole author of his misfortune. His pride as a producer of fine soft drinks was shattered. He had at least three messes to clean up.

His primary focus was to calm Mother; his second focus was to lure Marilyn and me back into the house and, lastly, he had to spend all of the final day of his weekend cleaning up the work of one day.

Dad never made root beer again. He gave away his few remaining bottles and capping equipment to Uncle Livesley, and even when asked repeatedly, he never shared his secret recipe with any of us.

Bradford and I share an appreciation for a cold beer on a hot summer afternoon. We drink our beverages straight from the can or bottle, savoring the different blends offered by foreign manufacturers or local microbreweries. However, around sunset on summer evenings I still long for some of that home-made root beer.

Chapter 2
MR. VARGA

One of the people I remember most vividly was Joey Borkowski. He owned and managed the drug store on the corner of Black Street and David Road almost directly across from our brown bungalow. Joey's Drug Store was a magical place where we could purchase exotically flavored popsicles (banana and root beer were my favorites) from the freezer and select the latest comic books. If we were really flush with money from odd jobs in addition to our weekly allowance and wanted to forego our trip to the Saturday matinee, we could order something from the soda fountain.

At various times, Joey employed some of the local teenagers to do part-time work in the store and at the soda fountain. When my older brother Bradford was in high school he went to work for Joey. My sisters and I mostly weren't allowed to go to Joey's when Bradford was working. Both my parents were concerned that if the cash register didn't balance or items were unaccounted for "it would look funny"–like one of us had been dishonest or had taken advantage of my brother's important position. They were worried that Bradford would be blamed. Then too, Bradford couldn't possibly keep track of his sisters, especially the two youngest ones, and do his job too. No, better that we should avoid Joey's during the times Bradford was there. On occasion we could break the rule and go for popsicles, but under no circumstances could we beg my brother for "freebies" at the counter or loiter about the store.

Bradford didn't mind this rule in the least. One of the reasons he was eager for the work and always made himself available for overtime was to get away from the house, from Mother, and from his sisters.

Another character that I remember was Red. Red was an auxiliary policeman who guarded the pedestrian crossing at the intersection of Adams and Black Streets. Marilyn and I attended John Adams Elementary School on Adams Street but had little reason to need Red's assistance crossing the busy junction, as our house and Adams Street were both located on the same side of Black Street. Mother was quite happy with this fact, but, nonetheless, cautioned us never to allow Red to assist us in crossing should the occasion arise. She thought we should rely on ourselves to get across the street. Red, I learned when I was older, acquired his nickname from the alcohol-induced rosacea that had turned his face, especially his nose, into a brilliant scarlet. In later years, I realized that Mother was quite right in assuming that we were better able crossing the street safely by ourselves than relying on Red's uncertain assistance.

Most of our neighbors also qualified as interesting–The Erickson, Smithson, Rockford, Carpentiere, Cavelli, Peterson, and Winthrop families all came from different places. English was the language of instruction and play for children, but at home the Carpentieres spoke French, the Cavellis spoke Italian, and other families spoke their native tongues. Most of them attended church on a more or less regular basis with the majority of them belonging to one of the Roman Catholic parishes whose growth could be correlated with the arrival of different émigrés from their respective old countries.

Among all these individuals Mr. Varga stood alone.

Mr. Varga owned the meat market next door to Joey's. Although Mother traded at Varga's fairly often because his store was convenient to our house, she wasn't always thrilled about doing so. Neither were some of the other families living on our block. They were put off by Mr. Varga's blood-stained butcher's apron and the floor and counters of his shop that were better viewed on a cloudy day. They also believed that Mr. Varga's meat was over-priced for its quality. Only in acute emergencies did any of our neighbors go to Mr. Varga's store.

The big attraction of Mr. Varga's store for me was that Mr. Varga always kept a full, if not-too-clean, cookie jar for the neighborhood children.

Mother never allowed me to accept a cookie from the jar, nor was I ever allowed to ask anyone, including Mr. Varga, for such a treat.

"You have plenty to eat at home," she told me firmly. You'll spoil your dinner, and you know you aren't allowed to have cookies between meals."

As soon as I was old enough to join the gang of kids that roamed and played from Cameron Street to Leominster Terrace and back along Black Street my older siblings warned me to stay away from Mr. Varga's store.

"You aren't allowed to go there," each of them told me repeatedly. "Mother doesn't think it's a good idea for you to be hanging around the stores. Go play with your friends."

But the Siren's call from the cookie jar pulled me to the store.

I began to think about how I could get into the little meat market without getting caught. After much deliberation, I began to manufacture reasons to go to Joey's. I would pass by Mr. Varga's after I finished at Joey's. Surely if I passed by the front door of Varga's Meat Market often enough, at some point Mr. Varga would invite me in for a cookie. Of course, these trips had to be carefully planned around Bradford's work schedule at Joey's, my school schedule, and the prying eyes of my older sisters. Thinking another person to help scout out the situation and keep watch over my planned sojourns might be useful, I shared my scheme with Spike Peterson, my best friend. Spike's mother had no compunctions about his accepting a cookie from the jar, but she was one of those people who didn't go to the little butcher shop very often either.

We laid our plans.

Spike astutely pointed out that we would need to be very careful since normal little kids didn't tend to hang out at the corner butcher shop unless their mothers were inside. Consequently our excursions were few and far between. Even so, we thought passing by the front door of the store at even irregular intervals might result in a treat.

Unfortunately for us, my older sister Marilyn began to notice that my trips to Joey's not only were more frequent, but also were ending without any visible purchase. Her reporting this to my mother resulted in a review of the rules about not frequenting Joey's Drug Store unless we planned to buy something there. No kid growing up in my mother's household was going to become a panhandler of treats at the local drug store. Mother had no idea that I was thinking of treats coming from Mr. Varga.

For several weeks afterward Spike and I steered clear not only of Joey's, but also of the entire corner. Then one day an unexpected opportunity to reopen our efforts arose. Spike, Hannah Winthrop, Mirielle Carpentiere, and I were playing in Hannah's yard when Mirielle's mother suddenly called us to her back door. Had we been playing too roughly for her taste? Mirielle was, after all, two years younger than Hannah and I, and three years younger than Spike. We had tried to be very careful with Mirielle who was small for her age, but maybe we had done something wrong. So we obeyed Mrs. Carpentiere's summons with some trepidation.

"Non," she answered us in her rapid Quebecois French-laced English.

"I want you children to go to Varga's with Mirielle and buy some ground beef. Mirielle is too little to go alone, so you can help her."

Hannah wasn't allowed to cross the street without an adult or her older sister with her but Spike and I agreed to go with Mirielle to Varga's.

As we approached the store, Mirielle became somewhat fearful even though her mother had written the order down and all we had to do was give the list to Mr. Varga, pay him for it, and carry it back to the Carpentiere's. She had never been sent on such an important errand before and was worried about making a mistake.

"Don't worry," we told her, "there are three of us, and Mr. Varga is really nice. He might even give us a cookie from his cookie jar."

In spite of this, Mirielle was still a bit nervous so as soon as we entered the store Spike spoke up. "We're here to trade," he said. "Mrs. Carpentiere sent us to buy some meat. Mirielle has the money to pay you."

"What kind of meat do you want?" asked Mr. Varga.

"A pound of ground beef," we responded in unison.

"A pound?" questioned Mr. Varga. "A pound of meat won't feed a family of six hungry people."

He reviewed the written instructions we handed to him.

"That's what Mama said we could afford this week." Mirielle's voice was little more than a whisper. "We can't buy more. Papa is sick and doesn't work right now, so we only buy a little."

"Well, never mind," said Mr. Varga to himself as he wrapped the meat in white butcher's paper.

Even as he worked, Spike and I recognized that he was packaging more than a pound of ground meat. We had been to stores often enough to recognize the difference between one pound of ground meat and more than one pound of other kinds of meat. Mr. Varga took a long time over the Carpentiere's meat order. When he finished he handed three large packages over the counter. Before Spike or I could ask any questions, Mr. Varga said, "I packed some bones for your dog."

"We don't have a dog," Mirielle whispered. "We don't have any animals except a cat."

"Never mind," said Mr. Varga. "Your mama will find a use for these."

And then, finally, he asked, "Would you kids like a cookie?"

The miracle had occurred! Mr. Varga had offered us a cookie!

With each of us carrying a package and munching a cookie, we left the store and returned to the Carpentiere's house. After delivering the goods, Spike and I bade Mirielle and Mrs. Carpentiere goodbye and left for our respective homes deeply puzzled by what had transpired.

"Why," I asked Mother when I arrived home, "would Mr. Varga give Mrs. Carpentiere dog bones when Mirielle doesn't have a dog?"

Mother answered carefully but with her usual directness. She wasn't thrilled with my accepting a cookie so close to mealtime. "You'll understand when you're older. Now go wash your hands. Supper's almost ready."

Shortly after this episode, Mother, Dad, Marilyn, and I left for Ohio. I never saw Mirielle, Spike, Hannah, or Mr. Varga again. But, over the years, I do know that I received something from Mr. Varga far more important than a cookie. I know now that one of my first lessons in generosity, goodness and community justice didn't come from Sunday school or church or any of my teachers or even my family. It came from a butcher of eastern European heritage helping a French Canadian family in a working class neighborhood within a large U.S. city.

I have often wondered how Mr. Varga knew the number of people Mrs. Carpentiere had in her family. I am still curious about how many other families who bought meat from him also received bones for their non-existent dogs.

Chapter 3
THE CLEAN ROOM MANDATE

"You kids live here too," exhorted Mother. "I'm not here just to cook your meals, do your laundry and clean up your mess. I'm not a servant; if I were, I'd seek better pay than I'm getting. You need to pick up after yourselves and take care of your own rooms. I have enough to do."

"Besides," Mother ranted on, "taking care of your own rooms will help you develop a sense of belonging to the family and an understanding of what it means to be responsible. Each of you needs to make your own bed and help out with the cleaning."

Mother was at her best when lecturing her kids and organizing her household.

Decades later I came to believe that Mother had attention deficit disorder. Certainly she exhibited the showcase spectrum of behavior: a rigid adherence to order and structure in all aspects of her life (and ours), an unpredictable and often violent temper, difficulty with computational work, compulsive talking, and little comprehension of social cues. This didn't work out well for her or for us, but it certainly made for an interesting, if chaotic, existence. On the occasion of The Clean Room Mandate, as I later called this era in our lives, Mother was both well-intended and completely clueless regarding the five of us kids.

With the exception of the night that she and Adela stacked the dirty supper dishes in the basement laundry tub so they could convince Mother that their assigned work was complete and they could go to the early evening showing of the latest movie, Grace gave Mother little trouble in the arena of housework. Grace herself was compulsive and orderly with her personal space and possessions. She shared a room with Adela who had much more relaxed standards of neatness. But since Grace was the eldest and Adela was the quintessential middle kid who had learned the importance of compromise and negotiation, they got along tolerably well with each other. Their room was always clean and tidy and met with Mother's approval.

Marilyn and I shared the other girls' bedroom upstairs. Marilyn was almost as fussy as Grace and was so impatient and critical of my efforts at bed-making and dusting that I simply turned my chores over to her in order to save time for both of us.

"You're going to redo it anyway so why should I bother?" I asked her. As a newly-minted five year old, I was both pragmatic and more than a little lazy.

Marilyn conceded the point, and for a long time, I remained not only chore free but also in good standing with my mother regarding room maintenance.

Only Bradford remained out of line. Since he had gone to work at Joey's Drug Store, his small room off the kitchen had become somewhat minimal by Mother's standards. Years later he told me that little difference existed between his mornings in army basic training and mornings at home during The Mandate.

"They get you up early," he enumerated, "and they yell at you a lot. You keep your mouth shut, do a little bit of what you're told to do, don't offer excuses, go your own way eventually, and you get through the day and go to bed with everyone mostly happy."

Unlike Marilyn, who stood upright in Mother's beacon and whose foibles lay bare to everyone's eyes, and Grace, who was equally vulnerable, Adela and Bradford were adept at living below the radar. They had either inherited or learned certain behaviors from Dad. They were calm, easy-going and patient; and owing to significant experience in bailing Marilyn and me out of a variety of situations, they could rationally think through most of our many family crises.

They were competent problem solvers and could also delegate well. In fact, Bradford was a master at delegating. Perhaps this skill set was refined because he was the only boy sandwiched in among all us girls, but however he grew his talents, he could easily convince a farmer to shear a sheep, card the wool, spin the yarn, knit the sweater, offer it for sale, buy it back, donate the money to Bradford, and make it all seem as if the farmer thought of it first. Whatever social skills my mother lacked, my brother possessed tenfold. Occasionally this particular skill would backfire, as it did a few months after The Mandate was enacted.

After considerable thought, Bradford worked out his room maintenance problem.

Since he was a man of means, he would hire one of his sisters to change his bed, dust the furniture, and mop the floor every week. The rest, he figured, he could get by with as long as the bed was made and his clothes (both clean and dirty) were stuffed into a drawer or closet. Mother's inspections only occasionally took her as far as bureau drawers or closets.

The next step was to identify the right sister to do the job.

Although Adela could be trusted not to tattle, her housekeeping was done largely under Grace's exacting tutelage. Marilyn and I were out of the question as housemaids. Marilyn could neither tell lies nor keep from Mother's scrutiny for long, and I was far too young either to complete a simple chore without supervision or to understand the significance of high-level business negotiations and the consequent need for confidentiality.

Through this process of elimination, only Grace remained. Not only did she appreciate the income, but she could be counted on to be very discrete regarding Bradord's plans. Most importantly she was an enthusiastic housekeeper. So Bradford went to Grace with his proposition. If she agreed, he would pay her fifty cents a week to do his assigned housework. In addition she was sworn to absolute secrecy.

Within two hours the rest of us kids knew everything about Bradford's and Grace's business dealings. Gone was the wholesome discipline Mother had tried to create so righteously.

By the end of the first week, Bradford had no chores at all. I was only required to dry the dinner dishes every other day and to keep my mouth shut tight about Bradford's and Grace's agreement. Grace and Marilyn were in control of the girls' bedrooms, and Grace had a steady, albeit small, income cleaning for her older brother. We were all relatively happy with the structure we created for ourselves, and no one told Mother or talked about it.

One evening at dinner she commented, "Everyone seems to be pitching in like I asked. You see how much smoother the household runs when we all work together and everyone does a share."

Mother not only believed in directing an occasional nugget of positive reinforcement our way, but also she was puffed up because her educational plans regarding her children had worked out so well.

She kept to this topic at length with only occasional requests to Dad to slow down his eating.

"You girls," she went on, "have kept your rooms nice and clean, but your brother sets the example for all of you."

Grace mulled over this statement. She was ecstatic that she had met Mother's high standards but somewhat bemused why Bradford had been held up as the epitome of good works when both his room and her own were equally clean. However, she remained silent.

Winter in New England came early that year. Bikes gave way to sledding and tobogganing down the hill at our local golf course. Ice skates replaced roller skates, and our trips to Buzzards Bay and Grandma Harrington's cottage on the shore were suspended because of the snow and cold. Our rooms were clean and tidy. Mother remained blissfully unaware of our arrangement until one particularly frigid Saturday in late November.

Grace had faithfully "done up" Bradford's room that morning while Mother had been upstairs attending to some other tasks. Thinking that the linoleum needed to be washed, Grace carefully mopped and rinsed the floor, and then she closed the door. Bradford was at work, and finding an immaculate room and newly scrubbed floor would surely arouse Mother's suspicions given that the inhabitant of the room had been elsewhere for three hours. Grace planned to open the door before lunch, to give the room its final airing, and Bradford would find it in pristine condition when he came home from Joey's.

Unfortunately, Grace forgot to open the door.

That afternoon Bradford arrived home unnoticed by any of us save Grace. She was hanging around the kitchen allegedly manicuring her nails but in reality waiting to be paid. Two quarters exchanged hands and Bradford proceeded to his room.

He immediately launched into a triple axel that would have made an Olympic skater green with envy.

What I heard was a tortured "AARRGHHH! OOOWWWWW!" followed by a WHOOSH, a WHUMMPP, a resounding crash and deathly silence. Bradford had spun around, launched himself into the air, flown over his bed and landed flat on his back on the floor.

Grace had failed to remember that Bradford's little bedroom had once been a kitchen pantry. Insulation was non-existent and the room's only heat source was shared from the radiators on the first floor.

Because the door was closed, the freshly washed floor had frozen into a perfect skating rink.

Mother was livid with a rage that lasted well into the evening.

It didn't matter that Bradford was in considerable pain and probably sustained a concussion. Mother's neat plan of instilling discipline on her wayward brood and organizing her household tasks was a complete shambles. Bradford sat at the kitchen table with a hot water bottle on his back and an ice pack on his head. Grace, sitting opposite him, was remorseful for causing him pain but still clung to her final pay. None of us had the nerve to tell Mother that her plan had been scrapped almost as soon as it left the dinner table several weeks before.

Grace's brief career as a cleaner for Bradford ended.

Grace and Marilyn maintained charge of the girls' bedrooms. Mother eased up a bit on The Mandate. Bradford survived the event with no ill effects and convinced Mother that helping his sisters develop a work ethic and earn a little extra money was an important task in which he should always assist if he was able.

Chapter 4
FROGS

"Your mother is going into the hospital for a while," Dad told Marilyn and me one day in early spring, "and while I'm working, Grace will be in charge of you. She's going to need your help with the chores, and you need to listen when she asks you to do things and when she tells you not to do things."

Dad spoke with unusual firmness.

Years later, Grace shared with me that she wasn't overly thrilled with becoming a housemother to her three younger sisters. This was partly because she was forced to give up her job at Lerners and her much valued income. It meant losing a position and colleagues that she genuinely enjoyed. Dad had promised to pay her for her work at home, however, and he was desperate for someone to keep things on a more or less even keel so he could continue working while Mother was out of commission.

Bradford and Adela who were in college and high school respectively needed no supervision. Other than keeping up with the cooking and cleaning, Grace's primary job was keeping Marilyn and me in bounds and out of trouble. One fine day shortly after Grace had taken over her new duties, we pestered her to allow us to go to Greenleaf Park allegedly so Marilyn could look for moss to make a terrarium.

Greenleaf Park, spanning 735 acres on donated land, was one of our most preferred places in the entire city. Every Christmas season we looked with wonder at the animated holiday lights which extended for miles throughout the park, including the zoo. In winter we learned to ice skate on the duck pond. In summer we played in the wading pool and had picnics at Massasoit Stockade. Sam, Marilyn's Labrador retriever, loved to run within the acres of pine and birch trees and swim in the ponds and lagoons. We rode our favorite ponies, Daisy and Dusty in the pony ring. The very best part of Greenleaf Park was The Birch Dale, a wild and woodsy glade that jutted directly into our neighborhood about four blocks west of our house.

The Dale, as we called it, was not a play-place condoned by anyone's parents or teachers that I knew of and certainly not by mine. Mother and Dad considered this area to be dangerous, harboring who-knew-what. For one thing, a little kid could get lost in there, or kidnapped by a stranger, or fall and be seriously hurt or worse. The trees were close together, the hills steep, the brooks filled with slippery rocks and hidden deep pools. Small kids like me were well advised to stay out of the Birch Dale altogether, and bigger kids were only allowed to go there in groups.

Marilyn and I loved the Dale.

Grace knew that the Dale was off-limits for us, and she never thought that we might be heading toward our forbidden paradise. She sighed and thinking it might be easier to allow our foray than to have us underfoot while she was preparing supper for Dad's arrival home from work, gave in to our request to go to Greenleaf Park.

"Don't go near any of the ponds or the Birch Dale," she told us. "I don't want you falling in and coming home wet, muddy, or with any stray animals."

The entire family knew my habit of falling into puddles, brooks, lakes or any body of water that was within a five foot radius of my short and sturdy legs. And Grace especially knew Marilyn's propensity for collecting reptiles and amphibians, although Marilyn herself drew the line at snakes. But for a young woman who had acquired considerable experience bailing Marilyn and me out of various scrapes, Grace was extremely naïve.

"Don't you tell Grace about the peanut butter jar," Marilyn ordered me as soon as we were out of earshot. "She'll know we're going to the Dale."

"But," I answered, "I thought we weren't allowed to go to the Dale."

"We aren't," Marilyn said simply. "But that's the best place to capture tadpoles and frogs. Just don't fall in and get wet or dirty."

She gave me a dark look. "If you stay out of the water, no one will ever know where we've been. If you say one word about this, it's the last time I'm taking you anywhere with me."

Marilyn often found the five and half years between our ages extremely irksome. She viewed me as more pest than companion much of the time: a perception that was mostly accurate.

We headed for one of the quiet areas along the brook's edge, intent on catching a few tadpoles that were abundant in the still, slow waters so we could watch them morph into leopard frogs.

After an hour or so of effort, we found no tadpoles, but Marilyn was able to capture four fully grown leopard frogs and secure them in the peanut butter jar, whose lid she had thoughtfully punctured with an ice pick (whose use was also forbidden) to provide air holes.

We headed home triumphant. I had managed to remain mud-free and dry, and Marilyn had a catch any kid could be proud of as well as the moss that she had gathered to stave off any questions at home.

We were full of ourselves.

During supper that night, a meal served promptly at six and for which no one was ever late, Mother's absence was keenly felt. When present she normally was the keynote speaker. While my mother was notoriously economical in all other aspects of her life and ours, she was not sparing of her conversation. She loved to talk, and mealtimes were her special platform. On this particular evening, our meal had been an unusually silent one. Dad tended to pay strict attention to his supper, and Grace, being tired from her rigorous cleaning, cooking, and laundry chores, was very quiet. Only when she left the table to get the left-over pudding and hard sauce keeping warm in the oven did Dad ask us how our day had gone.

Marilyn answered truthfully, "I was chosen for the school safety patrol. After school I took Mary with me to look for moss at Greenleaf Park."

Being the youngest, I didn't add anything, having learned at a very early age that the less I said about my doings, the more I could actually do without anyone noticing.

"Did you stay away from the brook?" Dad asked.

Marilyn mumbled something into her hash and potatoes while I contrived a discreet silence. Dad didn't have quite the same compunctions about the Dale as Mother did, but he most certainly wouldn't approve of the four captive leopard frogs that were residing securely in the peanut butter jar under Marilyn's bed.

Grace announced that she had a date that night with her current boyfriend, Robert Monroe. After the evening dishes were finished under her supervision–it was Marilyn's turn to wash, and my turn to dry–Robert came to walk Grace to the movies. Marilyn and I didn't care so much about dating, but we were rather jealous that Grace always seemed to see the latest movies at the expense of her dates while we had to earn and save our allowance dimes, wait until the Saturday matinee, and hope we could hit a cowboy feature preceded by a cartoon.

In retrospect, Grace deserved to go out with nice boys like Robert. She was dainty and petite like Grandma Harrington, with dark chestnut colored hair, a mouth that hinted at her sensitivity, large hazel eyes like my father's, and beautiful hands and nails. She had the Harrington sense of humor, that we all shared, and was a good listener, as well. She had also inherited Mother's need for order and Mother's relatively short fuse.

As soon as Grace and Robert left, Marilyn and I retreated to the upstairs bedroom we shared.

"What are you doing?" I asked her.

"I'm putting the moss in the blue dish," she said.

Mother had given her a large, blue ceramic dish to use for a terrarium and to keep turtles in. The turtles had escaped back into the wild, and Marilyn's first effort at keeping moss ended with the moss burning out. The dish, Marilyn thought, needed to be replenished.

"Now," she added, "I'm going to put the frogs in the bathtub. They need more room to swim around."

She was right about the frogs wanting more room, but had failed to acknowledge one critical fact. The bathtub had no cover.

Bedtime on school nights in Summerfield was universally observed across the city. This had been brought about by a conspiracy of the PTA and school principals all of whom seemed to agree that by 8:00p.m. elementary school age children should be promptly sent off. By 8:05 I was tucked in for the night, and by 8:30 Marilyn had joined me. After our foray to the Dale, we slept soundly.

Grace was supposed to be home by eleven on weeknights, a requirement which she found particularly galling since she was out of school and close to "being of age." My parents cared little about her frustration. In true New England fashion, the family rules were established along with our identities when were born and no negotiation was allowed about either rules or identities. Eleven o'clock remained her curfew.

Dad had to commute to Connecticut for work. Therefore by ten o'clock that night, he turned on the front porch light for Grace and went to bed after assuring himself that his domicile was in order and his small fry asleep.

Sometime between midnight and one o'clock that morning, a bloodcurdling shriek rang through the house, followed by another louder and fiercer harpy-like scream. A series of rapid footsteps followed.

"What was that?" I asked Marilyn whose bed was on the other side of the room.

"Hush," she said, "pretend you're asleep. This has nothing to do with you."

The shrieking increased in pitch and intensity. From what I could discern from deep under the blankets the agonized scream was assuredly Grace's. The other might have been Adela's.

"What happened?" I asked again.

At that moment Grace burst through our bedroom door in a fury, with Adela not far behind her.

"Girls!" Dad's voice was unusually loud. "Girls!! Hear! Hear! What's going on?"

"I went into the bathroom and at least two dozen damn frogs jumped out of the bathtub at me."

At the same time Marilyn piped in saying adamantly, "There were only four frogs, I swear it."

Marilyn's words, while true, were unnecessary in my opinion. I sighed. If she had only remained silent who could've possibly guessed how the frogs had entered our house.

Dad, somewhat suspicious, noticed that Grace was still fully dressed.

"Are you just getting in? Why didn't you turn the light on?" he asked her.

"I didn't want to wake anyone," said Grace truthfully.

I didn't blame her for trying to be discreet. If I'd been out after curfew, I thought, I wouldn't want to wake up the whole family, either, especially Dad who had to be up before dawn to go to work.

Her truthfulness, combined with Marilyn's, would have sent Mother into a towering rage if she had been home. Grace's yelling seemed to go on forever. She was incredibly upset about the frogs who had found their way into a bathroom that she had spent an hour cleaning. Why couldn't Dad or Adela have encountered the unfortunate frogs? They had long fuses, while Grace's was more akin to Mother's and at times could be measured by a one inch ruler.

"What are you doing out so late?' Dad asked Grace. He was probably less worried about the time than having been awakened so abruptly on a work night.

"I was with Robert," Grace defended. "We stopped for a soda on the way home, and then met up with Iris and Leo. Time got away from me."

By this time, she had pulled Marilyn out from under her blankets and had ordered her to go locate her frogs. After a lengthy pursuit—at the initial shock Grace had fled the bathroom and left the door open, frightening the frogs into full access to the house--and aided by Adela, Marilyn secured the last frog in the peanut butter jar.

"Tomorrow," said Dad wearily, "the frogs go back to The Dale."

Several months passed before Marilyn and I legally visited the Dale again. Much later, Grace overcame her shock and forgave Marilyn for her lack of foresight. Mother heard the whole story while lying in her hospital bed. Neither she nor Dad went to bed again before everyone else was accounted for and preferably in bed.

Eventually, Marilyn saved enough money to buy a small aquarium for her numerous catches.

Chapter 5
WESTWARD

"Well," announced Dad after his second trip of the month, "I think the position in Ohio has more potential than the one in Utica, so if Mr. Perini agrees, we'll be moving this summer."

Dad had just arrived home from Cleveland, Ohio, via the company plane. Marco Perini was Dad's boss at the aircraft plant, and I knew from dinner table conversations that Dad was up for a promotion and had been given a choice between a position in upstate New York or in Ohio. Mother was both excited and overwhelmed. How was she going to manage a move of such epic proportions? She would be leaving her extended family of in-laws, parents, older nieces and nephews, the familiar neighbors and friends, trades people, schools, parks, her church, and all the rest of her support system.

I had more immediate concerns.

"Where will we live," I asked Dad. "What about school?"

"You'll go to school in Ohio, near wherever we buy another house," Dad said.

I was mollified by this, but Marilyn had her doubts. As far as she was concerned, school was never good and probably never would be. For her, the saving graces of school were the sports teams and athletic programs, especially track and softball. What if she didn't make those teams in Ohio?

Initially Dad and Mother had more pressing concerns than settling Marilyn and me in new schools. Although Pratt and Whitney would pay for all our moving expenses and help Dad find a suitable house, Mother still had to help prepare our bungalow on David Road for the market and box all that she could for the move. But the largest and most wrenching issue for all of us was that Grace, who was already working full-time in a bank, and Adela, who had just finished her first year at Bridgewater State Teacher's College, had no desire to move to Ohio. They had opted for an apartment in Summerfield, which could, if they shared expenses, work out nicely. Adela had already dropped out of college and gone to work for an insurance company. Bradford had left for the army several weeks earlier prior to finishing his final year at Babson's. In one very short span of time, three of my siblings had left home, and although I did not know it then or accept the fact for many years, my sixth Christmas would be the last that the five of us kids would ever be together for the winter holidays.

When Mother informed Grandma Howes of the decision, Grandma was aghast. From her perspective any life west of the Connecticut River was highly suspect, and moving beyond the Hudson put people on the veritable frontier of civilization. Her response was certain and brief:

"You'll be scalped by Indians. The girls will be in a one-room schoolhouse with no indoor plumbing and will be in danger of rattlesnakes, wild animals, and unknown diseases. They'll grow up common and crude and without the influences of their older sisters, their brother or their cousins. And I know I'll never see any of you again."

Grandma Harrington was a bit more circumspect. Although she felt bereft by our planned departure, she had two sons in the greater New Bedford area, and two of her three daughters and their families were nearby as well. Also, her Quaker faith and calm disposition did not readily give itself to emotional displays. Nonetheless, she wasn't keen on the planned move to Ohio.

Dad and Mother had their own viewpoints. Descending from a long line of seafarers, Dad was born with a spirit of adventure, an appreciation for inventiveness, and an insatiable wanderlust that he shared with Mother. Having survived the Great Depression and the hardships of east coast habitation during World War II, they were both optimistic enough to believe that they could survive scalping and snakes. They were also practical enough to recognize that an economy transitioning from wartime boom to peacetime technology required some flexibility in career building. Neither Grandma Howes nor Grandma Harrington was able to convince Dad to stay in New England. He was going to Ohio, and therefore, his wife and two youngest children were going as well.

Dad made two additional trips to Ohio that spring to finalize his contract and job description and to buy a house. During his second trip, Mother and the real estate agent closed the sale of our beloved bungalow, and Dad found a ranch house on a large plot of land in a little farming community in northeastern Ohio. When he called home to tell us with great enthusiasm of the purchase, we all had many questions.

"What does the house look like?" asked Mother.

"It's not as big as what we have, but there's an acre of land for the girls to play in and lots of open space for Sam," Dad replied. "The house is a one story ranch, is only six months old, and has oak hardwood floors. The girls can have separate bedrooms."

Mother was ecstatic. She eagerly anticipated a vegetable garden, fewer complaints from kids about sharing a room, and no complaints from the neighbors about Sam-our escape artist disguised as a Labrador retriever. And she had wanted hardwood floors for a long time.

My questions were about school.

"Where will we go to school?" I asked for what seemed like the thousandth time.

"You'll be in the Claypool Local Schools," answered Dad. "The house is close enough to the elementary and junior high school so you can walk. By the time Marilyn is ready to start ninth grade, the new high school will be done."

Dad went on, "The kids here don't have nearly as long a school year as you do in Summerfield. They start after Labor Dad but finish by Memorial Day so they can help out on the farms. There are many large farms here."

Marilyn and I were feeling much warmer about school in Ohio. In Massachusetts our school year started on September 1 (unless it fell on a weekend) and ended on June 30th. In Ohio it seemed we'd have fewer weeks of school time.

"Just imagine," I told Spike on our way to school the next day. "We're moving to a ranch. I'll have my own horse that I can ride to school every day just like in the movies, and there'll be other animals and cowhands and everything!"

That day at school I informed Mrs. Grier, my first grade teacher, that because we were moving I'd need my school records immediately. This prompted a call to my house from Miss Abbott, the principal.

"Hello," she said, "this is Rose Abbott, from John Adams Elementary School."

Mother was used to these calls from Miss Abbott. Her first reaction was to ask, "What's she done now?"

Then Mother remembered that Marilyn was at Greenleaf Park Junior High School that year.

"It's about Mary," replied Miss Abbott.

"Mary?" questioned my mother, perplexed. I rarely had school issues, but if a call came it usually meant I was either bleeding or running a fever.

"She told Mrs. Grier that you're moving to Ohio and asked for her school records," responded the principal.

"We are moving," answered my mother, "but not until the girls finish school. I can't imagine why she wanted her school records at this point when she has over a month before the end of the term."

When I arrived home, Mother interrogated me regarding the strange request.

"If we're not going to live here anymore," I answered, "then I shouldn't have to spend any more time in school, should I? The kids in Ohio are almost done with school aren't they?"

My mother tried to reason me through this puzzle, but was only partially successful. When Dad arrived home, she told him the story, and his response to my confusion was simple and brief.

"When in Rome, do as the Romans do," he said.

The words, although wise, were to create much more of a dilemma than Dad realized when we arrived in Ohio and attempted to become Buckeyes with New England dialects, manners, and cultural habits.

I was disappointed about the school situation but dared not complain. Everyone else in the family said that Mother and Dad had enough to worry about without me fretting about school.

Those last days in Summerfield were an emotional jumble. Adela and Grace moved to their new apartment a few weeks prior to our departure. My grief was profound, but remembering in time that any open display of emotion would be met with little empathy, I dared not let anyone know how upset I was or how badly I felt. Yankee culture can be very cold and hard sometimes.

Hard, too, was the loss of Spike, Hannah, Grant, and Mirielle. Even Roderick, the boy who bullied me to the point where I cracked my toy guitar over his head, drawing blood and a quick phone call from his mother to mine, looked good to me. And Greylock... Greylock was an imaginary horse made of an old clothes pole that we younger kids took turns riding endlessly around the block. He was faster than any horse on television and more handsome than the real ponies we rode in Greenleaf Park.

The day we left Summerfield, Grace, Adela, the neighbors, and all the kids lined up to see us on our way. In the front of the group stood Spike, clutching Greylock.

"I'll take care of him," he called to me. "We'll miss you...come back and see us."

Off we drove through the streets of Summerfield, over the Connecticut River Bridge and westward to our new lives.

We took the New York Thruway as far as Syracuse the day we left Summerfield. All along the way, Dad explained about the interstate highway system, how and why the Thruway and other highways were designed and being built, and the relationship of the war effort and interstate commerce.

"Why," he said, "the President mandated that every five miles of interstate highways should be straight and level so planes can land there in an emergency."

Mother and Dad were big fans of the Eisenhower administration, and even though the every-five-miles-straight-and-level was patently untrue, planes can and have landed on these massive highways that emerged from the Eisenhower years.

I was fascinated by all this and also by the promise that we would stop at Niagara Falls on the way to our new home. That night we spent in a motel, my first ever, and after breakfast proceeded to the American Falls. We didn't have time to cross to the Horseshoe Falls in Canada. We needed to arrive in Ohio before the moving van did so Mother could direct the arrival and placement of all our furniture.

My first visit to Niagara was climaxed by two mini-catastrophes. The first of these was the discovery that my stuffed dog, Lassie, was left in the bedcovers at the Syracuse motel, and the second was the melting of a new box of Crayolas in 48 assorted colors on the back seat of the car. These events did nothing to decrease Mother's stress or my own carefully masked depression.

Late that July afternoon we arrived in Claypool. The house wasn't ready and our furniture was delayed. That night we spent in the Meadowview Motel on Brownham Road. Because of the nature of our situation, Marilyn, Sam, and I had an entire room to ourselves. True, it was adjacent to our parents' with a communicating door, but we had no beds to make, tables to set, floors to sweep, furniture to dust, or any other chores. Dad had to start work immediately, leaving Mother, Marilyn, Sam, and me at the motel. For two days the unlimited access to television, the endless rounds of Parcheesi, and our dish-free existence seemed like paradise.

"I don't know what else to do with them," wailed Mother. "I can't let them play alone outside or they'll be in the river with that dog."

By the third day, we were beginning to get bored with eating in restaurants and all the other luxuries. Finally, we begged Mother to let us outside longer than usual to exercise the dog. She relented, but we didn't stay long. Without sidewalks, trees, parks, hiking paths, playgrounds or other kids, the yard and parking lot of the Meadowview Motel were as barren as a Massachusetts beach in January.

On the morning of the fifth day, Dad finally took us to see our new house. It was about half the size of our old house and sat not on an acre of prime ranchland with stables nearby and horses grazing in a fenced corral, but on a quarter acre of mud, surrounded by an additional three-quarters acre of brush and wetlands. The yard looked like a swamp and came with a resident population of snakes, snapping turtles and frogs.

"Where are the horses," I asked out loud to no one in particular.

"What horses?" asked Marilyn and Mother simultaneously.

"Well," I reasoned, "if we're living in a ranch house, where's the ranch?"

Dad had a lot of explaining to do that day. In addition to the mud, the swamp, all the reptiles and amphibians that lived in the swamp, and the lack of horses, there was a lack of everything else. The driveway was unfinished, the garage non-existent, the neighbors uncommunicative, and the nearest grocery store of size ten miles away. No public transportation system existed, sidewalks hadn't been thought of, and the streets were unpaved.

Grandma Howes, I thought, may have been right.

The final straw for Mother came, however, when we entered the house.

"What's that smell?" she wondered.

Mr. and Mrs. Foster, who had moved into the house temporarily, were both teachers. They had purchased the house thinking they would be staying in the area, but found they couldn't earn a living on the salaries the Claypool Schools were paying, so they sold the house to Dad and prepared to move to another, wealthier school system.

"We raise chinchillas in the basement," replied Mrs. Foster. "They supplement our income."

"Chinchillas?" we girls queried in unison.

"Chinchillas are small animals that people raise for their fur," answered my parents.

"They look a little bit like rats," said Mother without enthusiasm. "But what I smell is more like rotten eggs."

"Oh, that," said Mrs. Foster. "That's the water. We have well water here, and the water is very hard. It contains a lot of sulfur."

"Is this what hell smells like?" I asked innocently. "In Sunday school we learned about hell, and it has sulfur and brimstone too."

"My God," murmured Dad.

What Mother said was neither reverent nor a murmur.

We spent another week at the Meadowview before the Fosters moved out of the house and our furniture arrived. On moving-in day, Mother sent me out to play. In one of her most ridiculous statements of all times she implored me to, "Stay out of the way, stay out of the mud, and stay in your own yard."

In roughly three minutes I was firmly stuck in mud up to my calves. After being roundly scolded for forcing my sister into the mud herself to come rescue me, I decided I had no place to go where I could obey all these injunctions. So I sat on the back porch as long as possible, and when I thought I might be in someone's way, moved to the front porch. Both porches were small concrete affairs that allowed room only for the dog and me. My disillusionment was complete. I had lost my siblings, my home, my friends, Greylock, my school, my extended family, my stuffed Lassie, and all my new Crayolas. I had no place to play, and I wasn't allowed to cry or complain. I had no idea what to do.

Although Marilyn and I had the separate rooms for which we had long campaigned, we opted to spend that first night together in her room. For one thing, my assigned space was pink, a wall color which I still abhor. For another, I was still in shock over the number of changes that had occurred in my life over the past month. Coping with disappointment and not showing any emotion had quite worn me out. I still needed to know that there was a body in the bed across the room. I fell asleep. Not, however, before hearing a heated argument coming from my parents' bedroom and not before listening to Marilyn crying quietly into her pillow.

Our new life, I mused much later, did not have an auspicious beginning.

Chapter 6
CULTURE SHOCK

Full summer came to Ohio in mid-July. The days were long, hot and humid. While Dad settled into his new routines at work and Mother began the laborious job of unpacking boxes, Sam, Marilyn, and I explored our new neighborhood.

Not many places were open for exploration.

Sam, much to the annoyance of the farmers whose dairy herds surrounded our neighborhood, found much enjoyment in chasing cows. Several of his cow chasing escapades resulted in telephone calls to Mother. After one particularly stinging conversation during which Mr. Benson threatened to shot that "black devil of a dog," Mother laid down the law.

"Sam has to be kept chained in the back yard and leashed when he leaves our property," she said. "We're hearing too many complaints from people."

Marilyn took this opportunity to begin walking Sam around the neighborhood. In 1956 the only streets in our subdivision were the one where we lived, a little street called Eugene Street that connected our street to the main north-south highway through Claypool, and Hoffman Drive. None of these streets were paved, but they were covered in large chunks of gravel to help control the dust. Walking and driving on them proved to be very difficult. A few houses were in the process of being built, but mostly our explorations consisted of visiting wetlands or fallow farm fields. These did not create a stimulating environment, but they did have a certain austere beauty, and Marilyn learned a great deal about dairy farming, cows, and swamps.

Other than my assigned chores of making my bed, drying the dishes, and dusting the living room, I was at loose ends much of that first Ohio summer. Because of this and because I was both homesick and lonely, I often went with Marilyn and Sam on their walks. Marilyn was lonely and homesick too and made no serious objections to having me accompany her on these treks.

The few neighbors we had thought this activity was very strange. Two kids wandering around the streets with a large black dog was unheard of. Word of this wonderment soon reached Mother's ears by way of Mrs. Andrews who lived next door to us on the north side and by way of Mrs. Parry who lived next door to us on the south side. Although Mother was offended by their comments, her only caution to Marilyn was to keep the dog off everybody else's property and ignore the gossip.

"What else can I do?" she complained to Dad when he came in from work. "The yard is still a sea of mud and the nearest park is six miles away."

"I'm working on the yard as much as I can," Dad defended.

This was true. Every evening after work he spent two hours clearing brush, killing snakes, and planting grass on our acre lot. He was determined to conquer the swamp and provide us with a lawn that would give us a play area and keep us and Sam in bounds.

The summer dragged on. Periodically we received letters from Grace and Adela who were reveling in their new-found freedom and from Bradford who was stationed in Germany. The sinking of the Andrea Doria off the coast of Massachusetts resulted in a flurry of mail from Grandma Harrington and the New Bedford relatives. Nobody in our neighborhood had any idea about how two large vessels could possibly have collided on a calm summer morning, and our explanation of how fog and currents worked in Nantucket Sound left everyone we talked to more confused. Furthermore, they thought Marilyn and I were putting on airs because we knew so much about fog horns and soundings and tides. Mother and Dad both tried to explain that we had spent so much time playing on the stony beach near Grandma Harrington's cottage that teaching us about these things was more a safety issue than "putting on airs," but the few neighbors we actually talked to were having none of their attempts at diplomacy. Soon Dad and Mother gave up.

After Labor Day, Marilyn and I started school. Mother had not had time to register us prior to the first day, so she walked with us to the principal's office. After a brief conversation with Mr. Wheeler, she delivered our school records and escorted me to my second grade classroom. Marilyn went to her home room in the eighth grade. This was our first experience in a school that encompassed kindergarten through twelfth grade.

None of us were impressed.

Mother was horrified that most of the elementary school teachers had at best two years of formal education after high school. She also was horrified by the suggestion that during the winter months Marilyn and I should ride the school bus to classes. After all, Mother reasoned, we only lived two blocks from the school which was less than a quarter of a mile away. In Summerfield, John Adams School was a full eight tenths of a mile one way, and we came home at mid-day for lunch and walked back to school afterward. Mother couldn't fathom why we should ride a bus when the exercise was so good for us and the school so close.

While Mother worked through her own misgivings and Marilyn was introduced to her eighth grade classmates, I struggled to understand my teacher.

For one thing, she was a short, very fat, gray-haired lady whose girdle was far too tight and pushed her ample bosom into highly improbable proportions. She carried a rolled-up newspaper, and as she waddled up and down the crowded aisles between our desks, she promptly smacked her newspaper alongside the head of any child who had offended her for any reason, however minor the infraction of the rule might be. She reminded me of an impatient dog warden dealing with a kennel full of wayward puppies. For greater offenses she had a wooden paddle in her upper desk drawer which she indiscriminately and liberally applied to various small backsides more and more often as the hot autumn afternoons wore on. She seemed like a lumpy and ill-tempered flour sack with a little head and squat limbs. Her blue-flowered dresses, of which she had many, supported this impression. Her disposition may have been positively inclined toward her small pupils, but, if that was so, I was unaware of it. I honestly don't think she liked any of us very much.

I know I didn't like her at all.

"Take out your tablets," the teacher ordered.

My only experience with tablets was that I wasn't allowed to touch any medicine or anything that looked like medicine without an adult's permission. And I certainly didn't have any tablets with me. I noticed all the other kids opening their desks and taking out sheets of yellow ruled paper. I didn't have any paper either. I didn't know what to do, and I was terrified that if I asked the teacher she would smack me on the side of the head. The newspaper hovered ominously nearby.

Fortunately, the little boy who sat behind me and whose name was Kenneth noticed my lack of paper and took two sheets from his desk along with a newly sharpened pencil.

"Here," he said. "Use these until your mother can buy you some of your own."

"Buy some?" I asked. "Doesn't the teacher give us paper?"

"No," he said. "You have to bring your own."

I was surprised. In Massachusetts the school provided everything we needed from crayons and pencils to paper and modeling clay.

"Write your names on the top of the paper," the teacher ordered.

"The top?"

I pondered which part of the paper was the top. Didn't the top depend upon which way a person put the paper on her desk? If the paper was placed lengthwise, the top would be different from the way it would be if the paper was placed widthwise. Should I ask? I turned around to see what others were doing. Kenneth had placed his paper lengthwise. But what strange marks he was making on it! Then I realized he was writing in cursive, not printing. In Springfield cursive writing didn't start until third grade, but fortunately I picked up a little of it from my older siblings. This was enough to get me through the writing of my name, although I didn't spell it correctly.

M-R-Y I spelled out in careful cursive. I didn't have any trouble spelling or writing my last name. In Massachusetts a person's last name was always more important than the first name.

The teacher came close to where I was sitting. I began to sweat, my heart raced, my head throbbed.

"M-R-Y isn't how you spell your name." she said.

"It's how I spell it," I responded.

I didn't reflect upon the fact that I must have sounded impertinent.

"The way you spell it is wrong," the teacher answered. "It's spelled M-A-R-Y. You forgot the A in the middle."

Remembering that Dad had said "In Rome we should do what the Romans do," I acquiesced. Dad had explained the saying to me and how important it was to try to get along with everyone even if they were different from me.

"Okay," I said.

And I wrote M-A-R-Y. And I wrote it again and again and again until the teacher was satisfied that I knew how my name was spelled.

The day wore on. In addition to needing paper, I discovered that I needed pencils, crayons, work books, glue, construction paper, a ruler, flash cards, a pencil sharpener, a gum eraser, and scissors.

I also learned at recess that while Kenneth was willing to share his paper and one pencil, he was less generous about sharing his playtime with me.

"I don't play with girls," he said. "Girls have cooties."

I had no idea what cooties were, but I was hurt by his refusal to play with me. More than ever I missed Spike. He and I had been the best of chums ever since I could remember. We always walked to and from school together, and if we had coinciding recess times at school we played together as well. And I had no idea what cooties were.

After recess we had a short share and tell session. All the other kids talked about what they had done over the summer, so I talked about moving to Ohio from Massachusetts.

"Where in Massachusetts did you live," asked one little girl.

"In Summerfield," I said.

"Is that near Boston?" the teacher prompted.

We had already become used to everyone thinking that anyone

from Massachusetts lived near Boston. Mother found this assumption particularly annoying, but Dad said we had to be patient and kind because lots of people really didn't know about anything outside their neighborhoods and we should try to explain things to them.

"No," I said. "Summerfield is on the other side of the state. It's near the Berkshires."

I couldn't imagine anyone not knowing where the Berkshires were.

"You mean the Berkshires, dear," said the teacher, emphasizing a long-sounding i in the second syllable.

"No," I said, "the Berkshires." Converting the i into a long e, the way I had said it all my short life.

"No, dear," said the teacher in an overly-kind voice, "the i is always long in that word."

At the time, I had no concept of phonics, long i's or long e's, but I did know how to say where I used to live and where, at the moment, I longed to go back to. But I knew the newspaper was not far off, so I said no more.

Marilyn picked me up at my classroom door that afternoon to walk me home. Previously she had not been thrilled with this assignment, but since we had moved, we had been exceptionally companionable. She was as depressed and dispirited as I was, and we walked home together avoiding the topic of school altogether. Mother had tea waiting for us when we reached the house. This was another custom that Ohio families never shared, but Mother was Scottish and Canadian by birth and upbringing, and tea in the afternoon was part of our daily ritual.

"Well," Mother asked, "how was your first day?"

"Okay," I said. I refrained from any further comment.

"Awful," said Marilyn. "This school doesn't have any sports programs."

Mother was aghast.

"What do you mean?" she demanded.

"No teams," said Marilyn. "At least not for girls."

"You're telling me the truth, aren't you?!" Mother exclaimed.

"Yes," said Marilyn. "No sports teams for girls. The school says that sports are unladylike, and girls are too delicate to play them anyway."

Mother exploded. She finally began to comprehend that we all might be on a cultural collision course with the local school system. Her rant about the backwardness of the schools, the lack of teacher preparation, and the idiocy of thinking her daughters were too delicate to engage in athletics lasted a good twenty minutes. She was preaching to the choir, but the choir was so disenchanted that even empathy was a lost cause.

At that moment, I asked my question.

"How do you say "Berkshires"? I asked.

Mother pronounced if for me, New England fashion, with the long e in the second syllable.

"You know that word," she said. "Why are you asking me?"

I followed up with my next question. "What are cooties? The boy who loaned me his paper and a pencil told me I had them because I was a girl."

"You don't have cooties," answered Mother. She didn't, however, tell me what cooties were.

I told Mother about the rest of my experiences in school that day, precipitating another rant on Mother's part that lasted through supper and beyond.

That night, as Marilyn and I did the supper dishes, Mother unburdened herself on Dad regarding the shortcomings of the local school system, the teachers, and little boys who said mean and untrue things about other people.

"Perhaps we should put them in private schools," he said.

"The nearest one is the Catholic school in town," replied Mother. "And we have no way of getting them there."

For Marilyn, school that year became a living hell. She made almost no friends, was continually laughed at and ridiculed for her accent, her speech patterns, and even her slim, boyish figure and short haircut. I felt sorry for her, but I could do little.

My own life that year was no picnic either. Although I had acquired some playmates among the little girls in my class, they weren't nearly as imaginative as Spike, or as kind and gentle as

Mirielle, or as smart as Hannah. They stood off from me whenever I suggested we play the games, sing the songs, and read the stories that were so dear to my companions in Summerfield.

Gradually, however, I began to adjust. I liked arithmetic, spelling and reading. I disliked penmanship, art, lunch, English, and phonics.

Phonics and English were a special trial for me. My teacher's English was as strongly accented as my own, only she spoke with the dialect common to people who had lived in southern Ohio most of their lives. During one phonics lesson she was teaching us the difference between long and short vowels.

"Ohio," she said, "has three long vowels. Who can tell me what they are?"

I was clueless. I could only discern two long vowels–the first o and the i in the second syllable. The way my teacher pronounced it was "Ohia." Unfortunately, at that moment she called on me.

"I heard two long vowels," I told her. "The first o and the i."

"No," she said, "the word has three long vowels. Both the o's and the i are long."

"But," I protested, "you said "Ohia."

"No," she responded, "I said, Ohia."

I was totally confused. Should I listen to what she said or say what I read?

Lesson after lesson continued like this. The word 'tiger' was pronounced 'tagger' leaving me wondering what kind of strange animal a tagger was. When she told us to "rid up" our desks, I had no idea what I was supposed to do. We were to "warsh" our hands often, but only with difficulty did I sort this out. A "rout" to me implied an army in full flight, but actually referred to state highway numbers which we pronounced as "root."

To be fair, my own dialect was not perfect either. An "idear" to me was more commonly said in Ohio as "idea". Most people say "modern" but Mother pronounced the word "morden". When we went to the store, we went to "trade", not to "shop".

But the toughest lesson of all was the pronunciation of the word "Worcester."

"Worcester," I told my teacher, "is a city east of Summerfield.

Sometimes we travelled through there on our way to my grandma's house."

Teacher sighed. I had pronounced the word the way all New Englanders pronounced it: as "Wooster."

"That word is pronounced 'Warchester,'" she said.

"It is?" I queried. "I've never heard it said that way before."

"Well," she said, "that's how it's spelled and pronounced."

Once again I returned home with a question about English. This time Dad was called in to manage the ensuing discussion. Even more so than Mother, Dad had an aversion to any kind of slang, sloppy diction, or mispronunciation of English. He toyed delicately with the word "Warchester" in his mind and finally answered me.

"You know that when you are in a place that is foreign, you need to respect the rules and the culture," he said.

I knew this because he had been saying this almost constantly since we left New England.

"Yes," I answered.

"What you should do in school is exactly what your teacher tells you to do. And what you should say is the way your teacher says it."

He concluded, gagging slightly, "Even if the word is 'Warchester.'"

"But," he added, "don't say it that way anyplace else."

Chapter 7
OH, CHRISTMAS TREE

"Christmas is just around the corner," said Mother one evening at the supper table. "What shall we do to celebrate the season?"

Adela and Grace already had decided to come to Ohio for Christmas, and I was invited to participate in a Christmas pageant put on by the Sunday school in the little church we had started attending that fall. Beyond those two events I avoided thinking much about Christmas. Bradford was in Germany, and I didn't even want to imagine a Christmas without him helping with the decorations. He always hung the holly and mistletoe around the house.

Dad, however, had apparently spent a great deal of time thinking over his holiday plans.

Having recently been reading articles in one of his camping journals and <u>National Geographic Magazine</u>, both he and Mother were developing an environmental consciousness that was years ahead of the mid-fifties.

"This year," Dad asserted, "we're not going to a store lot for our Christmas tree. We're going to have a live tree from a nursery."

"Aren't all trees living?" I wondered.

"He means a tree that we can plant in the ground," Mother explained.

I didn't know that live trees could be brought into the house. As I ruminated over the Christmas tree proclamation, several questions formed in my mind. Where would we put our gifts if we didn't have a Christmas tree in the house? I envisioned opening gifts in the backyard as a snowstorm raged. In addition to Bradford's total absence, and Grace's and Adela's presence guaranteed for only one short week, I was now coping with the loss of my favorite holiday tradition which was putting up the Christmas tree. A large hole expanded quickly in my seven-year-old heart.

"What about decorations?" I asked as I fought back tears.

Good little Yankee kids never openly displayed emotions. Doing so was ill-bred and untoward according to Mother. Besides, a kid with a major crisis was inconvenient and wasn't on any of Mother's to-do lists. Crises destroyed Mother's equanimity.

Seeing that an additional explanation was necessary to avoid a full-scale melt-down on my part, Mother continued to explain.

"We'll bring the tree into the house with the roots attached to it. We'll put it in a pail in the living room and decorate it as we always do. Then, after Christmas, we'll put away the ornaments as usual and plant the tree outside."

My relief was palpable. At least my favorite colored bell ornaments could still go on the tree. I redirected my attention to my apple pie. On Saturday nights in late fall Mother often served warm apple pie with a dollop of ice-cream on top and a slice of cheddar cheese on the side. Not even a discussion about a Christmas tree would put me off my favorite dessert.

Marilyn persisted. She was not as easily bought off by apple pie as I was.

"Why a live tree?" she asked. "Why not a tree like we've always had?"

"Because," answered Dad, "killing trees to celebrate a holiday for a few days is wrong and destroys the environment. This way we'll have a tree for the holiday and then help the environment as well."

Mother followed up with a lengthy lecture about Celtic Druids in the British Isles, Saturnalia in Rome, and the origin of Christmas trees in Germany, all in an effort to make Marilyn and me understand that Christmas was as much a pagan holiday as a Christian one. A Christmas tree saved was one more tree growing in the world rather than one more tree sacrificed to a holiday that was overly commercialized and had, in Mother's and Dad's mind, always been so. As Mother lectured, Marilyn and I remained silent and disapproving.

I was still somewhat confused about why my parents would want to plant a tree after spending most of their spare time during the past summer clearing the scrub saplings from the back of our acre lot to plant grass. But I knew better than to argue the merits of a standard green Scottish pine tree. The Christmas tree discussion was over for the season.

We were getting a live tree and that was that.

Although Mother had packed a large box of gifts, candy, cigarettes, and soap for Bradford and sent it to Germany many weeks earlier in careful accordance with the instructions for military mail, the pre-Christmas countdown for Marilyn and me began the Friday after Thanksgiving. Marilyn began to make plans to move into my room so Grace and Adela could share her room during their visit.

I began my own campaign to put up the decorations.

"When do we get the tree?" I asked Dad for the umpteenth time.

He suppressed a sigh in response. "Not yet. We have to go to the nursery and order one. Then we have to wait for the nursery to tell us the tree is in. Then we'll go to get it."

That Saturday we started to look for a place to order the tree. I don't know how many nurseries we went to, but Dad put a fair number of miles on the old Hudson over the next three weeks trying to find one that was open and either had a live tree or was willing to order one. Most of the nurseries were closed for the season, and the few that were open told Dad that purchasing and planting a tree was usually done much earlier in the year, with some people preferring spring and others autumn. People didn't usually plant trees, even evergreens, in the middle of winter. If we wanted a live tree, we should have placed an order in August or early September.

So said the final master gardener from whom Dad had begged to purchase a tree. Nonetheless, he finally sold Dad the only evergreen tree he had left in stock, along with a list of instructions about how to plant it after the holidays.

"Good luck," he said as we left.

As we left the parking lot with our first live tree, I glanced through the back window of the car and saw the gardener shake his head in disbelief.

The gardener was not the only person in a state of disbelief.

I had never in my short life seen such a Christmas tree as we had.

A blue spruce, it might have topped out at three feet, with a handful of scrawny, prickly branches. It came with a round root ball wrapped in canvas, and instead of the fragrant odor of balsam firs or white pines, it smelled of damp peat, earth, and cat pee. The two tops were canted to one side, and its colors were multiple shades of green and brown.

I was so wrapped up in my own disappointment that I couldn't even feel sorry for the tree. I had no problem understanding why nobody had purchased it during the planting season. However, as Mother and Dad pointedly informed us, it was a Christmas tree that we could plant after the holidays, and many other children in the world would be very happy having such a tree.

Arriving home, Dad plopped the tree root-ball-first down into a large pail of water and set it outside the backdoor.

"When will we bring it into the house and decorate it?" I asked.

"After your sisters arrive. The tree can't be in the house too long or it will go into shock and die. We don't want to kill it."

Grace and Adela weren't scheduled to arrive until the 23rd of December which was a week away. Every afternoon as Marilyn and I entered the back door after school we passed by the little tree standing forlornly in its bucket of frozen water.

Finally, the last day of school prior to our one and a half week holiday was over. Marilyn was more than ready to take a break from the daily ridicule of her classmates and from Mother's on-going harangues regarding her grades, her inattention in class, and her negative reports from teachers. I looked forward to a fortnight away from rolled up newspapers, daily phonics lessons and endless vocabulary drills.

Mostly I danced around the house ecstatic over the pending arrival of Grace and Adela who would be in Ohio in time to see my first performance in a Christmas pageant and to help put up the holiday decorations.

Even though I wanted to go with Dad and Marilyn to pick up Grace and Adela at the bus station, I had to be at the church early to prepare for the pageant. Dad dropped Mother and me off at the church with the promise to return with my three older sisters as soon as he could. As part of the Angel Choir I was to sing "Away in the Manger" while Mary, Joseph, and Mary's baby doll occupied the altar. That song was followed by "O Little Town of Bethlehem," "The First Noel," and "We Three Kings." With such significant duties to fulfill, I couldn't wait to show off my musical talents.

Grace, Adela, Marilyn, and Dad arrived just in time to take their places in the pew Mother had been saving.

When I looked up from my music book and saw them, only the stern warning I received earlier from Mother prevented me from leaping off the altar and racing down the aisle. I satisfied myself with frantic waving even though I knew I'd probably be in for a serious dressing-down for such an unseemly display.

My life, at that moment in time, was golden.

The next morning Dad brought our tiny bedraggled tree in its metal pail into the house and placed it on what had once been a fine old oaken library table. Not, however, before Sam took one sniff, noticed the distinct feline odor, and lifted his leg on the tree, thereby marking it as his own.

A cry of dismay from Mother, a sharp word from Dad, and exclamations of disgust from Grace and Adela did not in any way eliminate the smell of damp earth, peat, or cat to which Sam had added the smell of dog.

I think that at that point in her life Mother decided she was ready not only to dispense with Christmas trees in the house, but also with Christmas itself.

Her time of torture was not over.

The pail in which the little tree resided had a multitude of pinprick-sized holes in the bottom which Dad hadn't noticed. Within thirty minutes, as the ice-encased tree defrosted, the wood on the table was soaked, the new carpet was soaked, the floor-length drapes in which Mother had taken so much pride had wicked up some of the dirty water, and the entire living room smelled like the lion house at the zoo.

"Don't let the lights touch! Don't let the lights touch!" hollered Mother for what seemed the twentieth time.

The annual tree decorating had not even started when this mantra began.

Touch what? And why? Mother's fear of fire and electricity compounded during the Christmas season. While she never argued the beauty of Christmas lights in other people's homes, she would have easily dispensed with this beauty in our living room had Marilyn and I not been around. Mother listened obsessively to the radio most days, and every night she watched the local news shows on our newly acquired television with equal fervor. One short commentary on tree safety during the holidays was all that was needed to launch her into a panic regarding Christmas lights, trees, and hot bulbs touching evergreen branches.

Two hours later the single strand of lights was finally arranged to Mother's satisfaction with every one of the limited number of the tree's branches stripped of a significant number of needles to accommodate the "nothing touching the branches or needles" rule. The tree, not only scrawny but also newly bereft of half its needles, was almost bald.

We didn't need much additional time to place ornaments on the tree. With a flourish, a Santa Claus ornament was added to the taller of the two tips. After a final check to make sure no bulbs were touching any branches, we plugged in the lights. Mother proclaimed the virtues of the tree—"really it looks quite nice now that it's decorated"—while Dad, Grace, Adela, and Marilyn said nothing.

I marveled at how anything so wanting in traditional standards of beauty could draw so much attention from Mother.

Finally the great day arrived! Marilyn and I opened our stockings as soon as we were awake. Much to my delight I found a small wind-up toy that hopped and skittered across the floor, new crayons, barrettes for my hair, and an assortment of other delectable goodies. Marilyn had received things more appropriate for her age: a new hairbrush and comb, candy treats, a small tube of lipstick, face powder, and some delicately scented soap.

After a light breakfast, we all gathered around the tree, entirely hidden behind a mountain of presents. We had board games, books, pajamas, a new red-haired doll for me that came complete with her own wardrobe, and the crowning gift of all--new, warm, navy blue corduroy jumpers for school with long-sleeved white blouses and red sweaters for Marilyn and me, and sheets and towels for Grace's and Adela's apartment.

Mother had planned a traditional Christmas feast for us in true New England style that included roast turkey, cranberry juice and sauce, peas and carrots, mashed potatoes, pickles and olives, Waldorf salad, boiled onions, acorn squash, and lashings of sage and onion stuffing with pies for dessert. The meal ended with salted nuts, mint creams, and a box of chocolates to pass around.

The odor from the tree permeated the entire house as we ate.

All the following week we sisters enjoyed one another's company. Grace and Adela helped Marilyn and me open our new games. We enjoyed endless rounds of Parcheesi, checkers, Monopoly and some sort of geography game whose name escapes me now, but which I very much enjoyed.

Throughout the entire time the smelly little tree stood sentinel. Finally, the time came for Grace and Adela to return to Massachusetts. The day after they left, we took the decorations and the lights (much to Mother's relief) off the tree. Dad went outside to dig a hole on the north side of the driveway. Unfortunately for him, he hadn't planned for the frozen, rock-hard clay soil of an Ohio winter.

No spade, however strongly wielded, could scratch the surface of our front yard. Dad spent most of that afternoon with a pickaxe trying to create a hole large enough to accommodate the root ball of the tree. Eventually he succeeded, plopped the tree into its new and permanent home, watered it, and came inside to a supper of open-faced turkey sandwiches and left-over mince meat pie.

He was a very satisfied man and went to bed that night serene in the knowledge that he had provided a very good Christmas for his girls without violating the environment in any way.

The blue spruce didn't survive the winter.

With roots frozen in a pail, the shock of being carried into a warm house only to be anointed by an undisciplined dog, stripped of its needles, and then taken back outside and planted in a large and icy hole was too much for it.

Mother and Dad were profoundly disappointed but not defeated.

Every year following that first Ohio Christmas, they ordered a tree from one of the local nurseries to serve us through the Christmas holiday. Dad did wise up in some regards, though. He dug the hole prior to the first heavy frost of autumn and, in accordance with the first gardener's recommendation. pre-ordered the tree. But each and every year the trees failed to survive their early January planting with one exception.

When I was twelve and in the seventh grade another blue spruce tree was carried into our living room and placed on the battered old library table. Even uglier than the first live tree Dad bought, it too was anointed by the dog, stripped of needles in order to accommodate the string of lights, and then placed in its prepared hole on the north side of the driveway. Miraculously, this tree lived. It grew into one of the tallest, healthiest and most beautiful blue spruces in the community. Fifty-four years have passed and that tree still stands there today, a magnificent testament to my father and mother, who never gave up trying to make the world a more environmentally sound place for their children, grandchildren, and great grandchildren.

I have had fifty-four more Christmases as well...most of them made rich and sweet by the blessings of family, friends, love, and generosity. Even though my siblings and I are separated by miles and age, we are not separated in our hearts. Now the greatest gifts we exchange are telephone calls, updates regarding children and grandchildren, and the memories that have so enriched our lives.

Chapter 8

CAMPING

"If we're going to travel for your entire three week vacation, we're going to have to find the means to do so."

Mother pronounced another edict at the supper table, one which would have a profound impact on all of our lives, especially the lives of us four girls and our future spouses and children. I was hoping to return to the Harrington's family compound on Mattapoisett Pond near Cape Cod. But even though Marilyn and I treasured our time with our cousins, aunts, uncles, and grandmother, Mother had not enjoyed the constant cooking, cleaning up, laundry or long afternoons sitting alone while the rest of the family watched Aunt Atherton's new television.

"The family and Mattapoisett Pond," she said, "are not much different from being at home. Besides, with all the older kids gone, where would be the fun for Marilyn and Mary. All anyone wants to do is watch television, and I get bored with that."

Mother did not approve of us watching television. She thought we should be playing board games or reading if we weren't going to be swimming in the pond. In retrospect, she was probably right about our missing Grace, Bradford, Adela and the older cousins, but I wasn't ready to accept the huge change in our lives that came from our moving on and the older kids moving out. Even though my adjustment to life in Ohio had been marginally easier than Marilyn's, I still silently grieved for the city and friends I had left behind and the family members scattered throughout New England and Western Europe.

In spite of Dad's prediction that Grace and Adela sharing an apartment would not last longer than one month—no doubt he was remembering the endless squabbling of their years sharing a room while at home—their partnership had flourished, and they were more or less happy in their tiny second floor apartment. We all missed them. Both Marilyn and I thrilled with the hope that we might go back home for a visit to see them. But Mother and Dad had firm control over the family finances, and if we were going to travel, our plans needed to fit with the money Mother had carefully saved over the past year.

After mulling things over for the entire spring, Dad finally came up with a solution to which Mother enthusiastically agreed.

We would try camping.

The camping experience, which Dad conceived of after a series of conversations with Hunter Thompson, one of his colleagues at work, resulted in Mr. Thompson loaning us a tent and some equipment to try for one weekend. If we decided we liked it, we could use it for our first lengthy trip.

After our initial weekend in the tent, Dad and Mother discovered that they were campers and travelers born for the road.

Having become dedicated to the idea of roaming the country for three or four weeks every summer, Dad decided he wasn't very comfortable borrowing someone else's gear and began thinking about investing in his own equipment and a basic set of campground tools.

A garden of both new and second-hand camping equipment began to sprout in the extra garage bay. Mother's and Dad's excitement grew as rapidly as the quantity of stuff: scratchy wool blankets purchased from the Army-Navy surplus store, air mattresses, two boxes of Melmac dishes, stainless steel silverware, an assortment of pots and pans, plastic dish pans, towels and washcloths, followed by suitcases filled with clothes for hot weather, cold weather, and in-between weather were augmented by cases of canned soups, meats, and vegetables. Mother believed in being prepared for any kind of emergency.

The pieces de resistance were two small flashlights—one each for Marilyn and I to use after dark.

"Remember," Dad cautioned, "flashlights run on batteries. Don't use them unless you need to or you won't have them when you most need them."

Dad might as well have given us an outright order to read our comic books under the bed covers at night.

Meanwhile, Mother made lists.

She had clothing lists, meal plans, equipment storage blueprints for the garage and basement, flowcharts to assure efficiency in setting up and breaking camp, and duty assignments for everyone in the car. She then drew a schematic for the trunk and top carrier of the car and conducted timed packing drills to establish schedules for when we set up camp and when we broke camp. Not only did she want us to be a team, but she wanted us to be so in record time. No United States Marine Corps drill instructor was more efficient than Mother in training her raw recruits.

One Sunday afternoon as he was reading the paper, Dad exclaimed, "I've found a tent for us! See this advertisement?"

He showed the newspaper to Mother.

"For sale," she read out loud. "At Sears. Over-stocked umbrella tents. Fifty dollars."

"That sounds like a good deal," she observed.

The next day she and Dad came home with the tent. Dad was very pleased that he had been able to bargain ten dollars from the requested price.

"Shouldn't we try to put it up?" Mother asked.

"Okay," responded Dad. "We can put it up in the backyard."

The following Saturday he and Mother spent the forenoon wrestling with the tent while Marilyn and I stood by waiting for our assignments and watching the hill of canvas unfold to its full potential as a family shelter. Dad explained that the tent, just as its name implied, had an internal frame that raised and lowered like an umbrella. The frame blossomed out from the center pole that was inserted in a small grommet in the middle of the tent roof. The internal frame drew the ceiling taut, which was supposed to prevent water from pooling on the canvas and creating leaks. Dad shared this information with the lofty air of a seasoned camper.

Our tent, when erected, did not resemble an umbrella. It did not, in fact, resemble anything that I recognized.

For one thing, the frame kept sliding up and down the center pole, apparently because of a missing latch that held everything in place.

"Not to worry," Dad said. He was very upbeat. "I can jerry-rig an external support with a piece of aluminum and a screw."

At this point Mother, who had significant experience with Dad's attempts to fix things, looked somewhat dubious.

The tent appeared to have been inexpertly sewn together. No matter how high or firmly Dad placed the internal frame, all four corners of the tent sagged significantly. He worked feverishly to remove the sags corner by corner, but as soon as he corrected a particular corner, another sag in another corner replaced it. His frame adjustments were accompanied by a constant raising and lowering of the tent roof which resembled the unsuccessful efforts of a large bird attempting to fly. We kids had learned from experience that some parental efforts were better left without sharing our observations, so we stood quietly by while Dad worked through the mechanics of the tent.

Finally, he conceded that, evidently, the tent was not quite perfect but would certainly be adequate for our need and would serve us well enough.

"And," he added, "it only cost us forty dollars."

"No wonder we paid so little," Mother commented.

"We should go camping for a night or two," said Dad, "to identify anything else we might need prior to taking a longer trip."

Looking around at all the gear stacked in the garage, I couldn't imagine what else we possibly needed, but then, I was only eight and my opinions didn't count for anything.

The afternoon prior to our first weekend trip with our very own camping kit, Mother, with packing chart in hand, supervised Dad's loading of the Hudson. Judging from the quantity of food she selected for our overnight trip, she apparently thought we would not be home for several months and that no grocery stores existed in eastern Mohawk County. When the car was packed, Marilyn almost had enough room to cram herself into the back seat. I had my choice of either sitting on a case of Snow's clam chowder or lying prone on the ledge below the rear window. Because I had experienced a growth spurt that summer that went unrecognized by Mother or Dad, I could no longer fold myself onto the ledge, so I opted for the chowder.

The weather forecast for that night included cold temperatures and the potential for heavy rain.

Arriving at Cherokee State Park, we checked in at the camping office.

"Plenty of tent sites are available tonight," the park ranger informed Dad. "You can drive around and pick one, or if you prefer, I'll assign you a site now."

He looked askance at our vast equipage. Marilyn was wedged in among the food, I sat elevated on the chowder with my head squished into a window, and blankets were stuffed everywhere. I'm not certain, but I think I saw a flicker of a smile pass over his face. We were obvious first-timers.

We rode around the park for what seemed to me to be a very long time looking for the perfect place. Mother wanted something close, but not next to, the restrooms and showers. With two kids who had bladders the size of walnuts, she wanted to keep her escort duties to the restroom at a minimum. Dad was looking for a relatively flat spot for the tent. Marilyn, as the official water bearer, wanted a site close to the water pump, and I wanted someplace close to a fir tree so I could enjoy the smell. As we stopped to look at the available tent sites, the discussion about each gradually became louder and more heated.

"This looks good," Dad said.

Mother finally agreed with him. The site did meet three of the four criteria—no balsam fir was in evidence, but a sappy-looking scrub pine hung over the picnic table marking the spot. And we were close to the water pump and restrooms.

Up went the tent, sagging corners and all. Marilyn and I started to inflate the air mattresses which was our first task on the duty roster. Dad, after much wandering around in the woods, found a tree branch that he could place against the center pole to keep the frame in place. He had forgotten about permanently fixing the center pole almost as soon as he made his promise to do so. The air mattresses, blankets, sheets, towels, and clothing were moved into the tent just as the rain began coming down "with some vigor," as Dad put it.

A light supper of clam chowder and canned fruit supplemented with molasses cookies was hastily put on the picnic table. During this meal, as he dodged the downpour, Dad reviewed certain rules of campground etiquette.

"After dark, always use quiet voices," he said. "Waking other people is extremely rude. Don't shine your flashlights into anyone's campsite or tent. If you need to go to the restroom, walk as quietly as you can. And," he added, "be careful you don't touch the inside of the tent because you'll pop the air pockets in the canvas and cause a leak."

"Lastly," he instructed, "don't run into the branch holding the center pole or the whole tent will be down on us."

I didn't want to confess that, in my case, the campground was free from flashlight danger. I had already exhausted the batteries reading comics in bed after hours. I think Marilyn may have had some life left in her batteries, but I wasn't about to ask her. She would be sure to tell of my wrong-doing and I didn't want to get yelled at. The rest of Dad's little admonitions I took seriously.

We didn't have any kind of awning or canopy over the picnic table, so almost as soon as supper was over and the dishes were washed, we moved back to the car to play a round of canasta. After three canasta games and a cup of hot chocolate for Marilyn and me--Mother and Dad had something to drink with a little more substance to ward off the night's chill-- we squelched off to bed. Dad occupied the air mattress along the back, Mother had the front, and Marilyn and I each were assigned a side. I was cold, but good campers, according to Mother, did not complain. I was determined to be a good camper.

Around two o'clock that morning, the inevitable happened. The combination of cold, the rain drumming on the canvas tent, the clam chowder, and the hot chocolate forced me out of my nest of blankets.

I needed to use the restroom.

In spite of not having a working flashlight--why had I spent so many hours reading under the covers of my bed?--I was sure I could find my way. Dad's words echoed in my head, "Don't wake anyone up." As I jumped over Mother's inert form, I tripped over something behind me.

"Probably a pair of shoes," I told myself.

I unsnapped the tent door and poked my head outside.

Congratulating myself at not waking anyone, I opened the tent door fully and tripped again, this time over a small rock beside the tent door. I landed face down in a large puddle that had collected outside the door. Soaked to the skin, I trudged off to the restroom.

My pride in accomplishing an exit from the tent without waking anyone and finding my way in a strange environment with no guiding flashlight vanished on the return trip. Where was our campsite? I was sure I had made no wrong turns emerging from the restroom. What had I done?

As I continued walking toward what I thought was our campsite, my increasing anxiety was replaced by immense relief.

I had seen our car.

What I didn't see, however, was the unmistakable formlessness that was our tent. Where had it gone? I moved closer, fear and confusion again gripping my soul. Only when I arrived at the car did I see a violently wriggling hillock of canvas.

"Thurston!" Mother was yelling. "Thurston! Where are you?"

I heard a muttered and unintelligible response.

"Dad!" cried out Marilyn in panic. "What's happening?"

"The tent fell down," I heard him say. "The branch supporting the center pole came loose."

I knew then what I had tripped over in my triumphant leap from the tent. As I launched myself so handily through the door, my foot caught the branch supporting the center pole. My family was trapped inside, and I was outside, standing in a fine, penetrating drizzle.

"Where's Mary?" Mother had finally noticed my absence as she groped around the fallen tent.

"I'm out here," I answered.

I tried to sound brave, but I was really drenched, half-frozen, temporarily lost, and I was shivering with cold, shock and fear. I had committed a crime about which I had been openly warned and had no idea of what the consequences of my actions would be. I knew they certainly wouldn't be pleasant.

I sat down on the picnic table bench to await my fate.

The epic struggle of man versus tent continued. Hampered as he was by being aroused from a deep sleep enhanced by Southern Comfort and the misguided efforts of Marilyn and Mother, Dad made a valiant effort to get that tent back to its original position. The corners, which had served as collection points for gallons of rain water, let loose their load. The roof and sides began to cascade water onto Mother's blankets, the floor of the tent, some of the clothing (mostly Mother's) and Dad. Thirty minutes later, in a last ditch effort to win the battle, Dad pushed the center pole into what he assumed was the middle of the tent roof, hoisted it, secured it with the branch, and suggested firmly that everyone go back to bed.

"I thought I told everyone to avoid that branch," he said wearily.

"You did," Mother replied. "But what do you expect after a bowl of chowder and hot chocolate on a cold, wet night."

Mother behaved as if the clam chowder and hot chocolate was somebody else's idea. To me she asked, "Why didn't you ask someone to go with you? And why didn't you use your flashlight so you could see what you were doing?"

"You told me not to wake anybody up," I defended.

Dad sighed. "I didn't mean you shouldn't wake us up. Just other campers. The reason Mother's sleeping bag is in front of the tent is so you could wake her if you needed to go out."

Morosely I thought to myself, "I was just doing what I was told."

The next day dawned bright and cold. We awoke to the smell of wood smoke, frying bacon and onions, and faint whispering just beyond our campsite. A crowd of onlookers had assembled to check out the obvious disaster that had taken place the preceding night. Dad hastily pulled his pants on over his pajama bottoms and crawled sideways out of the tent. We followed after him one at a time, with Mother being last out the door.

The aftermath of the Battle of the Tent was clearly visible. Our canvas castle was half down with the supporting structure positioned squarely on the lee side forcing the tent floor in an upward slant toward the road of the campground. A small moat of water where a previous camper had trenched the area surrounded it. The door lay sideways on the ground.

"Hey, buddy," one of the crowd called, "you want some help getting that back up?"

Some people would have given up at that point, but Dad was never too proud to learn.

"I'd very much appreciate it," he answered. "As you can guess, we're new at this camping business."

Within a few minutes, aided by the group, the tent was up and airing out, our blankets were on a clothesline drying in the sun, and the pole had a permanent fix in the form of a small clamp screw arrangement improvised by a car mechanic who was camped in the site across the road.

We were ready for a second day. By the time we returned home on Sunday evening, both Mother and Dad were deep into planning an extended camping vacation.

Our first three-week camping trip, with a colorful assortment of equipment and two kids stuffed once again in the back seat of the car, was an ambitious tour of western Ohio, both the lower and upper peninsulas of Michigan, southern Ontario and southwestern Quebec, Vermont, Massachusetts, New York, and finally home. Details of the trip are not part of this particular chapter, and I will only say that my sharpest memory is of Mother's misfortune in developing a serious case of thrombophlebitis when we reached Vermont. While she recovered in the warmth and relative comfort of the Bishop DeGobriand Hospital, Dad, Marilyn, and I shivered in our tent during an unseasonably wet and drafty week.

Upon arriving home from that trip both Mother (with her foot and leg still elevated most of the day) and Dad were enthusiastic nomads.

They decided that camping was an inexpensive, fun way to enjoy the best part of traveling: making new friends in the various campgrounds and parks where we spent our nights, grocery shopping in local stores, meeting people in their own environments, and exploring geography and history. Marilyn was never committed to tenting around the country, but she rarely complained. I was too young to do anything but go along for the ride and absorb the experiences.

A few years later when Dad replaced the Hudson with a new station wagon, Marilyn and I defected from the tent and arranged our own sleeping space in the back of the car. Mother was happy to see us go. She made curtains for the windows to match our new, heavier sleeping bags. Our clothes were neatly rolled in waterproof knapsacks with each person responsible for his/her own belongings.

Over a five year period, we traveled thousands of miles in the station wagon, and Mother and Dad slept in their remarkable tent. We met a variety of people, made many friends, and, for three weeks each summer and many weekends, we cherished our nomadic existence.

Shortly after Marilyn graduated from high school, Dad purchased a beautiful new umbrella tent. He, Mother, and I became a threesome for four more years until I left home for college. As Marilyn's work schedule and her second career as a professional dog handler permitted, she joined us.

Mother and Dad probably never realized how deeply I grew to love tent camping and everything else about our trips. Our adventures fostered in me a great love of geology, botany and zoology, along with history, geography, anthropology, and sociology. I learned lessons beyond price. I am certain that these summer experiences added a depth to my education that would never have been possible otherwise.

The traditions continued on after I married. The first vacation my husband and I took after our honeymoon was an extended canoe trip through the Canadian wilderness. We were knowledgeable about camping and wilderness survival, and delighted in the two weeks of freedom from the routines of our daily lives, household and workplace electronics, highway travel, and urban light pollution and noise. Upon our return home we welcomed the obvious advantages of hot showers and restaurant prepared meals, but we both missed the quiet of the vast Canadian wilderness.

We finally stopped camping when we reached mid-life because of the limitations of our health. However, even though we now stay in hotels when we travel, keeping flashlight batteries functional is one of my chief obsessions.

Chapter 9
DISBELIEF AND BELIEF

"I can't see the board," I explained to Mrs. Chandler for what seemed like the hundredth time that week.

Amanda Chandler was my third grade teacher and I adored her. I would have done anything in my power to gain her approval. Unfortunately, we were doing addition that day. Learning how to "borrow" from one column to another escaped my understanding and not only was I becoming frustrated, but so was Mrs. Chandler. I couldn't see enough of what she was doing on the chalkboard to begin even a rudimentary understanding of the arithmetic lesson.

One of the hardest things about being a kid, I had come to understand, was that nobody seemed to believe me even when I was telling the absolute truth. I don't think that any of my siblings had tendencies toward habitual untruthfulness any more than I did, although the occasional omission of certain facts regarding our activities rendered Mother constantly suspicious and hyperaware to the point that she questioned the veracity of anything we told her. Since neither Mother nor Dad paid much attention when I told them I couldn't see the problems on the chalkboard I dropped the topic.

"Maybe," I told myself, "I'm not able to learn this."

After all, Marilyn had all kinds of issues with school, as did Grace before her. They seemed to be surviving just fine in spite of marginal marks in school and in Marilyn's case, ongoing behavior problems. Maybe I was more similar to them than I was to others in the family.

Fall was particularly beautiful that year. Dad had planted several maple trees in our yard the previous spring and though they were still saplings, their foliage kept up with maple tradition and varied from orange to brilliant scarlet. The flowers that Mother had planted in the beds bordering the south side of our yard had bloomed in profusion, and the purple of asters and cosmos, and the bright multi-colored zinnias could be seen the length of the street. They were the last things I saw in an impressionistic profusion of home as I turned onto Eugene Street towards school in the morning, and the first things I saw when I returned in the afternoon.

I walked to school daily with Regina who was one of our next-door neighbors. Regina was an occasional playmate whose interest in horses and western television shows rivaled my own, but other than that we had little in common. Still she was the closest thing I had to a friend in my after school hours, as most of my own classmates lived too far away for any social activities and she was the only other little girl in the immediate neighborhood.

The sixth week school reports came out in mid-October. Marilyn's report was barely acceptable. Mother's resultant rage, fierce beyond description, was the result of both wounded pride and something far more deeply rooted. All that things that Mother disliked about herself and that she so desperately tried to either disguise or deny came to vivid life in the form of Marilyn. I felt a vast pity for my sister, but also fear for myself. Although I had not failed arithmetic or penmanship, a mediocre grade was the first approach towards the slippery slope of failure. Would I too become the target of such rage? Marilyn's school issues became such a focus for Mother and Dad that my own progress was given a parental nod and a quick sign-off.

I was off the hook for another six weeks.

My daily struggles with arithmetic were mostly offset by my success in other subjects. I liked reading and spelling, excelled at memorizing facts and had a special love for social studies which we had begun that year. However, seeing the chalkboard became no easier. To placate me, Mrs. Chandler moved me to the front of the room.

"You can see better now, can't you?" she asked.

Her question was really more of a statement. She had not yet learned the difference between open or close-ended questions. Obviously the correct answer was yes.

"Yes," I said.

My answer was the opposite of true.

Mrs. Bannister, the school nurse, organized the in-school vision tests that year starting with the high school students and working down through the lower grades. Marilyn was identified early as one of the kids who needed additional screening by an optician. Within two weeks Dad took her to Dr. Spencer who prescribed glasses to correct her vision.

A month later as my third grade class lined up for vision screenings, Mrs. Bannister walked past us carrying a large board with a strange mixture of numbers and letters. She paused for a longish conversation with Mrs. Donnellson, another third grade teacher who was a special friend to many of the elementary school faculty and staff. Those of us waiting in line grew restless and bored. To entertain ourselves, my classmates and I began to scrutinize the odd looking board.

"What's that?" asked Sarah of her first cousin Rachel. Rachel and Sarah were two of my classmates who had great friend potential.

"That's how they test us," Rachel answered.

"You have to read the chart," she went on. "and if you get all the lines right then you pass the test."

"Well," I thought to myself, "I'm pretty good at remembering things and if all we have to do is memorize some lines I can pass the test."

Mrs. Bannister and Mrs. Donnellson finally concluded their visit and moved on to their respective duties with Mrs. Donnellson lining up her class in alphabetical order and Mrs. Bannister setting up the eye chart in the hallway where we were going to test.

Our class followed Mrs. Donnellson's. When my turn came I passed with flying colors even though I couldn't see a thing on the chart from where I was standing.

I had memorized all of it when Mrs. Bannister and Mrs. Donnellson were talking.

Mother was vindicated, Mrs. Chandler remained frustrated by

her inability to teach me arithmetic and Dad was relieved. Glasses were expensive and he already was paying for his own, Mother's and Marilyn's.

"I think I need glasses too," I told Mother when Marilyn arrived home with her new glasses.

"No you don't," she answered.

Her voice was firm and final.

"You only want them because your sister has them. You passed your initial screening with no problems at all."

I sighed inwardly. Maybe I did have some other problem that prevented me from doing arithmetic and made people not believe me.

I gave up the battle.

The following Saturday, Regina and I were playing cowboys in the vacant lot between our house and the Andrews. A large oak tree, felled when the well was drilled on the corner, served as a horse. Our play grew more intense…an imaginary telephone rang in the pretend ranch house that was a second and larger oak tree. I ran full tilt to answer the call. No doubt the sheriff was calling to announce that outlaws were headed our way and we should take all precautions.

I put on an additional burst of speed with Regina screaming ever more loudly behind me and closing fast on my heels. Only a few more yards to go! We ran as if our Keds were on fire.

I crashed headlong into the oak tree.

Regina was hysterical, alternately laughing at the sight of her playmate running full speed directly into a large and very visible tree and screaming at the horrific sight of my broken nose and blood-covered face. She drew the attention of my parents and older sister.

Marilyn picked me up from the ground, helped me into the house and laid me on my bed. Mother, who failed to see the humor in any of the situation, was yelling loudly at Regina and promptly sent her home, never to return to our yard again. Marilyn thought I had just done the dumbest, most stupid thing in the annals of childhood.

"How could you have run into anything that big?' she asked.

I was too shaken up and hurt to answer.

"I spent the rest of the day in bed with ice packs on my head. Mother and Dad would not trouble a doctor with such trivia as a childhood accident, so the broken nose remained unset. The numerous abrasions, bumps and bruises were duly cleaned, treated with tincture of methiolate and left uncovered to the air.

"It's healthier," Mother said.

"You'll heal more quickly."

The thought of raging infections or future disfigurement didn't occur to either parent. Going to the doctor was not on the to-do list that day.

The following Monday I walked to school alone. Regina would never be my playmate again. Her mother was highly offended at Mother's outburst blaming her for my accident.

My face was a variegated blend of purple bruises, red healing abrasions and bright orange methiolate. I looked and felt badly beaten up. When Mrs. Chandler asked me what happened I answered, truthfully, that I had run into a large tree while playing. Her response surprised me.

"Come with me," she said.

"Where are we going?" I wondered to myself.

That question was quickly answered when we went to Mrs. Donnellson's class across the hall.

"You see, children," said Mrs. Donnellson.

She stood me in front of her entire class.

"This is what happens to boys and girls who don't take time to tie their shoes when they are playing. They trip and fall. If you don't want this to happen to you, always, always tie your shoes properly."

I was devastated. I tried to explain what really happened, but Mrs. Donnellson quickly shushed me.

"Never mind, dear," she said in her kind teacher voice.

"I'm sure it won't happen again."

Apparently the truth of the situation was evident only to me. No one could or would believe that I hadn't seen something as large as an oak tree.

Finally, however, one person took matters into his own hands. Shortly after my tree-bashing episode, Dad called Dr. Spencer and scheduled an appointment for me to have my vision thoroughly checked. He and Mother were mortified by the result.

"Your daughter," said Dr. Spencer, "has a serious astigmatism and significant myopia. Her uncorrected vision is so bad that she is legally blind. I'm surprised you and her teachers didn't recognize the problem a year ago."

I was proven truthful, but took no joy in the realization. Mother helped me pick out the frames for my new glasses. The first morning I put them on I wept for joy.

"I can see," I told Dad.

"I can see everything so well. I can see the flowers and the trees, and the grass and the television. I can see everything and it's all so beautiful!"

Dad told me that one of the greatest gifts I would ever receive in my lifetime was my sight. He knew I was grateful for the glasses.

I could've sworn I saw a tear in his eye as I raced out the back door to look at the flowers in the border and the grass on the lawn.

Even though she lived next door, Regina never invited me to play again and Mrs. Parry never forgave my mother for her angry outburst.

Many years later, a physician diagnosed my breathing problems as mostly caused by a severely broken nose. He repaired the deviated septum that was a result of my vicious encounter with an oak tree.

Ironically, after we grew up, Regina Parry became a plastic surgeon.

Chapter 10
ADELA'S WEDDING

Adela and Angus were engaged!

Nobody could argue that Angus McLean would be a promising addition to our family. He was a gentle, kind and sensitive man, firmly rooted in all things domestic. He was later proved to be an ideal first brother-in-law, a devoted son to his aging father, a loyal and principled employee, a model husband to Adela, and a loving father to his children. I had known him most of my young life, for he and Bradford had been chums even before they left for college and were roommates at Babson College until Bradford left to join the army.

Angus and Adela started dating while Angus was at Babson. Prior to a college sponsored dinner and dance event, Angus agreed to "fix up" a date for Bradford. In return, Bradford asked Adela to be Angus's partner for the evening. Soon after, Angus and Adela began to date steadily. Mother was thrilled about this first engagement of one of her daughters and couldn't wait to tell Esther Appleton the good news and everything related to the upcoming wedding.

"Angus is an accountant with a large chemical firm. He's the son of one of Summerfield's finest families. His father owns a printing company, and the McLean family has always been active in church," Mother told Mrs. Appleton. Mother was full of pride.

"He's Scottish, you know," she added.

Being Scottish sealed the deal as far as Mother was concerned.

Mrs. Appleton was our back door neighbor. She, her husband Reuben, and their three children had purchased and moved into one of the first houses on Leah Street, which ran parallel to Reid

Avenue where we lived. As a neighbor, Esther Appleton was intensely interested in all goings-on. She kept tabs on every new house being built, every grass blade, flower, and tree being planted in the entire neighborhood and could tell you what was going on within every family. She was gregarious and shared all her knowledge eagerly. Born to observe, record, and talk, she kept everyone, from children on up, informed of all the neighborhood doings.

"The wedding will be in June, of course. Grace will be the maid of honor," Mother continued. "Marilyn is old enough to be a junior attendant. They'll look beautiful in blue dresses. Bradford can serve as the best man. He'll be able to arrange a leave of absence with his commanding officer and come to the states for the wedding."

The Cold War was at its height, but a family wedding trumped the increasing tensions between East and West Germany in Mother's plans. Mother was sure that Bradford's participation in the wedding would avert his possible deployment to the Middle-east which was a hot zone of increasing concern.

That Adela and Angus had their own ideas for their big day never occurred to Mother. Though this somewhat obvious oversight on Mother's part must surely have occurred to Dad, he wisely kept silent. He had learned long ago not to interfere with Mother's thought processes.

Like the outdoor temperature that winter, Mother's emotions ran up and down.

"They might have consulted with us first," she aggrieved. "Most girls talk with their mothers about getting married, and the groom should ask her father for permission to marry. They're awfully young for such an important decision."

Mother was going down the scale again, vaguely perceiving that maybe she wasn't nearly as in control of the wedding as she might have wished since she hadn't heard much lately from either Adela or Grace. Nonetheless, her plans moved eagerly along.

"Because the wedding is in June," she said, "the school year will be finished. We'll be able to camp and can stay in Massachusetts for a week or more and see most of the family and some friends."

I'm not sure that Adela had set a particular date for the wedding, but June sounded very promising to me. We hadn't really spent more than a day or two in Massachusetts since we'd moved. Owing to Mother's serious illness during the previous summer's camping trip, we were only able to stop briefly in Summerfield before returning home so Mother could rest and receive the medical care she needed. I was disappointed by this, although I understood that Mother had been critically ill. I wanted to pick up the threads of my life in my old home.

One evening shortly after the news we would be heading east in June, Mother and Dad arrived home from their weekly trip to the supermarket.

"I have a surprise for you," Mother said as she handed me a cardboard booklet.

Inside the booklet was a cardboard page of human figures carefully perforated around their edges for my small fingers to punch out. The figures included two men, two women, and a small boy and girl. The following pages contained several pictures of colorful dresses, suits, and shoes all with tiny tabs. These could be cut out with scissors and placed on the figures.

Mother must have had an ulterior motive.

She knew I loved playing with "cut-outs" as the little girls in my class called paper dolls. New ones like this didn't fall into my lap every week.

"These are wedding paper dolls," announced Mother. "You can play with them and practice being a flower girl so you'll do a good job in Adela's wedding."

"What's a flower girl?" I cut directly to the chase.

"A flower girl is a little girl in a wedding who leads the processional down the aisle of the church. She normally wears a very pretty Sunday dress and shoes and carries a basket of flowers. Sometimes she scatters baskets of flowers as she walks down the aisle."

Aha! A frilly, starchy, uncomfortable dress and patent leather shoes! Mother knew that I was strictly a sweatshirt, jeans, and sneakers kind of kid and had a particular aversion to overly fussy clothing. I only wore Sunday dresses if absolutely required. I knew that Grace, Bradford, and Marilyn would be in the wedding party, but I had no idea of my own involvement. A flower girl? My physical scars from the infamous encounter with an oak tree were barely visible, but my self-confidence was slower to heal. I was fairly certain I couldn't lead anybody anywhere, let alone a church aisle. For the moment, though, I accepted what was clearly a bribe. I thanked Mother for the paper dolls and took them to my room to start the assembly process.

Wedding plans in Massachusetts, very different from Mother's but on a parallel course, also moved on a-pace. Mother and Dad had been very clear with Adela that they had little money to contribute to a wedding. Consequently, Adela enlisted Grace early in the process to be her maid of honor and help keep expenses under control. This turned out to be an excellent choice, since Grace had superb taste in decorating and attire and was well-attuned to the budgetary restraints imposed by Mother and Dad. Angus's mother was also selected as a helper.

March arrived and Mother had begun to research campgrounds in western Massachusetts when the first bombshell dropped. The wedding date had been set for late April! Mother was incensed! How could she possibly make dresses for Grace, Marilyn, herself, and me in one month's time? An April wedding annihilated her plans for a week of leisure in Massachusetts and would require pulling Marilyn and me out of school for at least one day. It also meant that we'd be staying in a motor court rather than camping. Mother's disappointment deepened when Bradford wrote and told her that he would not be coming back to the states, and Angus would be selecting another person to stand as his best man.

While all this was going on, I grew increasingly anxious about my own wedding assignment. Would the time spent with family and friends offset the frills, lace, puffed sleeves, starch, and patent leather I would surely be required to wear? Could I walk down the aisle tossing baskets of flowers over the floor and the guests without tripping, falling or otherwise disgracing myself?

One day at recess Mrs. Chandler called me to her. I flew to her at her summons. In hindsight, I suspect Mrs. Chandler found playground duty tedious. To break up the monotony she often used her playground time sitting on the merry-go-round and engaging in serious conversation with her little pupils. My conversations with her were an early introduction to the Socratic Method of teaching, for she asked probing questions, for the most part, and was a good listener. On this afternoon I took the opportunity to steer the conversation wedding-wise.

"I have to be a flower girl in my sister's wedding," I told her. "I'm not sure I know what to do or how to do it. I'll have to wear a scratchy dress and shiny shoes and maybe a wreath on my hair."

I had earlier noted that my wedding paper dolls, at least the female figures, seemed to have scratchy dresses, veils and wreaths or hats.

"Maybe she thought you'd like to get dressed up. Being in somebody's wedding is usually considered an honor," said Mrs. Chandler.

An honor! I had never considered that being a flower girl was an honor. Maybe Mrs. Chandler was right! From this point on I was not only excited to be in the wedding, but I was also determined to be the best flower girl ever. I rehearsed all the moves in my mind and, finally, concluded that I wouldn't actually throw baskets as I walked down the aisle, but only the flower petals in the basket. And Mrs. Chandler had said that most weddings had rehearsals the evening before the event. I knew about rehearsals from being in the church Christmas pageant, and I had found them to be helpful in working out any little issues or hiccups in the performance.

I came close to regaining my self-confidence when another bombshell was dropped.

Adela wasn't going to have a flower girl in her wedding. She and Grace, owing to the logistics imposed by a six hundred mile gap between us and more importantly, the lack of financial resources, planned a pretty and simple chapel ceremony. Marilyn wasn't going to be a junior attendant either.

I can't say either of us was devastated, for Marilyn shared my distain for fuss, but I think Mother might have been. Her plans had totally unraveled. The final straw was when Adela and Grace together selected and purchased an ensemble for Mother to wear to the wedding and mailed it to her to ensure that the sizes were correct. The dress was lovely: light blue which brought out the vivid China blue of Mother's eyes. They had selected a matching hat and, of course, gloves.

Shortly after that Mother took Marilyn and me shopping for our dresses. She also insisted that we have short topcoats to wear in case the weather turned cold. My dress was a pink dotted Swiss and my coat a pale blue, while Marilyn chose aqua for both dress and coat.

The dress looked pretty but was as uncomfortable as any dress could be.

On April 18th we loaded up all our finery and drove to Summerfield. We left Ohio extremely early that morning in order to be on time for the rehearsal scheduled that night. After a ten hour trip (it might have been longer), we arrived in Summerfield, checked into the motel, and, as soon as we had changed into our second best clothes, drove to the church for the rehearsal. Mother wasn't keen on having me stay up so late, but nobody knew what else to do with me. In any event the instructions to me were quite simple…be quiet and stay out of the way.

I don't remember much about the rehearsal, but I do remember at some point afterwards we were at Angus's parents' house. Although Angus himself tended to be quiet, his father, whom most of us would later refer to as Grandpa McLean, was an outgoing and talkative soul. He really enjoyed entertaining, and that evening he was brilliant. He introduced all of us to the latest technology…a new Wollensack reel-to-reel tape recorder which he intended to use to record the entire wedding ceremony. We all had a chance to record our voices saying and doing different things. Mother and Dad practiced speaking into the recorder, while I sang a little song I had recently learned in school. What a wonderful time we had! We were very late getting back to the motel, and we had to be up early the following day so Dad could be fitted for his tux prior to the wedding. Our schedule was too tight to allow any visiting with friends or family until after the wedding.

The sun shone softly, almost like a yellowed pearl, that morning. The temperature, which is always chancy in a New England April, was mild. Adela and Angus couldn't have asked for better weather. We had to be at the church a good hour or so prior to the ceremony so everyone could get situated.

The New Bedford relatives began to arrive twenty minutes after we did. Uncle Dennis, Dad's older brother, and Aunt Marie, his wife, were there along with Aunt Ellen, Cousin Jean and her husband John. I don't remember if Aunt Eunice and Uncle Carl were there, but Aunt Briggs and Uncle Brendan were not as they had already moved to Florida. The New Bedford crowd were wonderful, down-to-earth people who quite often violated Mother's sense of propriety. Independent thinkers and doers, they paid little attention to social conventions. I hardly recognized them in their wedding finery. I was used to seeing them in the bathing suits, shorts, and cotton dresses that were the daily attire at Mattapoisett Pond.

As the family filed in with as much decorum as they could muster, Mother took the opportunity to lecture Marilyn and me once again regarding wedding behavior.

"Even though you aren't in the wedding, I expect you to act like ladies. Sit up straight, don't talk or whisper during the ceremony, and don't wriggle or squirm," she said.

She spoke more loudly during the first part of this little sermon than she needed to so Adela, who was within hearing distance, could receive her final pre-wedding message.

Having laid down the law to Marilyn and me, regarding proper wedding decorum, she wanted to do so again with all her in-laws. I give her lots of credit for her self-restraint as she greeted them warmly and without a single hint about their behavior.

Finally the ushers came for Mother and Marilyn while I tagged along behind Mother.

The wedding had begun.

As Grace began her walk down the aisle, I did whisper once to Marilyn, "I'm glad I don't have to do that."

Marilyn immediately poked me in the ribs and shushed me.

While this was going on, Mother became increasingly misty-eyed. Grace and Adela both looked stunning as they walked down the aisle of the chapel. Even though none of her plans had come to pass, the wedding was finally happening! So far everything was working out, if not exactly as Mother had imagined, at least satisfactorily.

Mother held her breath. The ceremony moved along. The Reverend Dr. Howard, who had served as the pastor of the Methodist church ever since Mother and Dad had attended there, conducted the ceremony with all the dignity his office afforded. He had a sincere love for all the members of his flock and held a special appreciation for children. As soon as the final pronouncement was over, we were escorted back down the aisle to form a receiving line.

Mother breathed a premature sigh of relief. For her, the wedding was over.

For me, the moment had arrived for a full melt down.

I was more than over-tired from the extraordinarily long drive and late hours, and I'd spent too much time in a dotted Swiss dress. I was profoundly disappointed that once again I had failed to reconnect with my life in Summerfield. I had been struck for the first time directly between the eyes with the harshest of all realities.

Summerfield would never be my home again.

As I approached the good Dr. Howard to shake hands as I had been taught (good Yankees never, never hugged anyone not in their families) I pronounced in bell-like tones, "My sister is a skunk."

Which sister I was referencing was not relevant. I'm not even sure I know now. I began a wild, uncontrolled keening. I was done with weddings. Adela was going away forever, and I'd never see her again. My family and friends in Summerfield would always be six hundred or more miles away. I didn't realize then what a wonderful brother-in-law I was gaining or that long-distance relationships were possible. Mother and Dad attempted to quell my unseemly and embarrassing outburst, but were unsuccessful. In the end, Angus and Adela talked with me themselves. They assured me that they were not really going anywhere except maybe to Ohio in the summer.

Their words were comforting to me, but what really won me over in the end was Angus's promise.

"We can read comic books together and we'll make fluffy-nutter sandwiches."

Who could deny a fellow lover of Superman comics or an exquisitely designed marshmallow fluff and peanut butter sandwich?

I can say now that Angus always kept his promises. The following summer he and Adela came for a visit, bringing their little daughter with them. He and I spent a gratifying time reading comic books and eating fluffy-nutter sandwiches.

Chapter 11
BEAN POT

Two years had passed since our move to Ohio, and Mother and Dad were increasingly concerned that Marilyn and I were losing both our regional dialect and our approved ways of behaving, as well as our cultural identities. We were neither Buckeyes nor wholly Yankees. After giving much thought to this, Mother came up with a multipronged solution. We would spend part of each summer vacation in New England, exploring all the places we'd never been to when we lived there, and Mother would continue to purchase and prepare foods common to New England tables.

Consequently one mid-summer's day when I was nine years old, Mother announced, "Saturday we're having a real clambake. We'll have roasted corn, green salad, steamed clams, a bean pot, and other good things like we used to have on the Cape and at Long Pond."

Neither Marilyn nor I had a great interest in either hunting for steamer clams or stuffing quahogs. What was the point of having a Cape Cod experience when our body of water was either Lake Erie, whose shore line was covered with dead fish, or a muddy reservoir that was still being built. Our "beach" consisted of the hard-packed clay soil in our back yard. All of our cousins and our two older sisters were still in Massachusetts, our brother was in Germany, and our grandmothers had no intention of coming to visit us in the uncivilized and uncharted Ohio country. Mother's carefully orchestrated event would include only herself, Dad, Marilyn, Sam the dog, and me.

Reality never mattered very much to Mother. Having made her decision, she first laid down the law to Marilyn and me regarding our participation and then informed God that the weather would be perfect for our clambake. Dad was charged with gathering driftwood and digging holes in the backyard on Friday night to accommodate the clams and bean pot.

"Do you ever remember us having a clambake in Massachusetts?" I asked Marilyn.

I could always count on her to fill me in on certain facts that Mother tended to omit or embellish.

"No," Marilyn said. "The only thing I remember about shellfish is the day that Elliot, James, Paul, and little Dennis gathered all the mussels they could find on the rock shore at Grandma Harrington's cottage and then threw them at me. They got into a lot of trouble for it. Rotten mussels really stink."

"You were too little to remember," she added.

Marilyn sounded somewhat bitter. Apparently she had had no one with whom to share her victimhood at the time this incident occurred.

The next day Mother and Dad began shopping for the items necessary for our immersion into our native culture. As my father later told the story, he and Mother first went to the meat department at Kroger's. With their Yankee speech habits of placing r's everywhere except in words that actually contained them, they quickly confused the meat manager. Dad asked if he could please have two dozen littlenecks.

"You want livers' necks?" queried the meat manager.

"No. I'd like two dozen littlenecks. They're clams." Dad spoke with the same patient voice he used with me when I was being particularly obtuse about something that was obvious to most people.

"We don't carry those," the meat manager responded. "Is there something else I can help you with?"

"What about quahogs?" Dad replied. "Do you have any of them?"

Quahogs are just another kind of clam. Dad was beginning to grasp at straws.

"You want a quarter of a hog?" replied the man. "We'll have to order it special and we price it by weight. Did you have a particular weight in mind? How big is your freezer?" He was trying so hard to be helpful and sell something to Dad that would approximate a littleneck clam or a quahog.

"Um," said Dad. He was completely confounded. "We'll just have a three pound chuck roast."

The meat manager was relieved and helped Dad select a nice roast.

"We can have it on Sunday," Dad said to Mother.

After a private consultation in the canned goods aisle, Mother and Dad decided to continue with their remaining list and look elsewhere for the clams. The A and P didn't have clams. Neither did the Claypool Local Market, nor the Ash Road Market where we could collect green stamps for ever so many purchases, nor any other store in the area. The search for fresh corn was no more productive, and in the end, Mother and Dad came home with a ham instead of clams, canned corn, the ingredients for the bean pot, and a small watermelon.

Dad arrived home from work the following Friday afternoon promptly at 4:30. Immediately after a quick supper, he changed into his yard and gardening clothes, grabbed his spade, and began digging the hole for the bean pot. As the sun blazed toward setting, Dad stripped off his outer shirt. Seeing him sweat profusely, Marilyn felt some sympathy for him and offered to spell him at the spade, but in spite of her considerable strength, she was unable to make any headway. I learned some things about clay soil that evening as well as some new vocabulary words that I was certain shouldn't be shared with anyone.

Esther and Reuben Appleton, our backdoor neighbors, came over to observe the process.

"Why are you digging a hole where you just cleared and seeded?" asked Esther. She seemed amazed.

Mother answered, "This is for baking beans."

Esther's jaw dropped. "Baking beans?"

"Yes." Mother sounded lofty. "We're showing the girls how to do a New England-style clambake."

Obviously baffled, Reuben and Esther slowly backed away from the small divot in the clay and retreated to their own house. We could see Esther peeking around her curtains from time to time checking on the progress of the hole. She and Reuben were relieved when Dad finished the hole late that evening. They wouldn't have been able to sleep until the digging was complete.

Forenoon on Saturday found the Hoffman Allotment, where we lived, humming with life. Most of the school-aged children were outside riding bicycles, jumping rope, playing tag, shooting up the streets with toy guns or else helping clean the family Fords and Chevys that were the standard for our little neighborhood. As I still had few friends among these other kids, I was helping in the kitchen. Mother mixed the beans, a jar of molasses, bacon, ketchup, and onions with the concentration of a chemist.

"Don't tell your father about the onions," she appealed to me as she stirred everything into a casserole dish.

"He detests onions, but if we dice them small enough, he won't even notice they're in the pot."

By the use of the pronoun "we," I became a co-conspirator in the onion sub-plot, and therefore equally responsible for Dad's discomfiture if a stray onion tidbit was discovered among the beans.

Flushed with success, Mother clapped a lid firmly on the casserole dish and carried it to the hole in the yard.

As Mother was formulating the beans, Dad, having given up on locating driftwood in our suburban tract, had built a rousing fire of discarded wood products from the new houses being built a block west of our plot. He added the weekly rubbish collected from the house and when Mother came proudly out the back door with the beans, Dad informed her that as soon as the fire burned down, he would rake back the coals, lower the bean pot, and cover it with dampened lawn clippings since we didn't have any seaweed to help make steam. Mother returned to the house to put the ham in the oven and decant the canned corn into a pan. Marilyn was assigned to find the ripest tomatoes in our vegetable garden. My job was to take Sam some place where neither of us would be in anyone's way.

"In order for the beans to cook properly," Mother explained, "they have to stay buried in the grass clippings for a very long time with the hot coals over them."

The rest of us engaged in other pursuits while waiting for the beans to cook, but Mother began to grow restless. Were the beans cooking as they should? Would they be ready when the ham was done? Were they drying out prematurely? Shortly after the clock struck eleven, Mother made a decision that would literally reverberate through the community and add to our already questionable reputations. Mother asked Dad to move the coals, take the earth from the top of the bean pot, and open the lid so she could add some water and check on the cooking process.

In spite of ourselves, Marilyn and I were very interested in what was happening. We approached the hole in the yard and watched as Mother added a teakettle's worth of water to the beans, carefully closed the lid, placed the pot back in the hole, covered the hole with new grass clippings—the old ones had been rendered down to a small pile of smoky ash—and replaced the earth and the coals.

Within three minutes the gates of hell blew open.

The bean pot exploded.

Beans, potshards, grass clippings, and coals flew everywhere. Remembering the duck and cover air raid drills from elementary school and convinced that the Russians had dropped a nuclear bomb in our back yard, I fled to the basement stairwell, followed by Sam. There we cowered wrapped in a sleeping bag. I imagined the worst.

My sister and parents were dead, killed by the nuclear holocaust. Would my brother ever come home from Germany? Would Grace or Adela or one of my aunts or uncles take me back to New England? I really belonged there anyway. None of us had ever fit into Ohio where people laughed at the way we talked, poked fun at Mother's insistence that we sleep with our bedroom windows open all winter, and openly despised our dog.

Of course, I would probably die anyway. Radiation poisoning, I had learned at school, was a terrible sickness and most little kids died from it. If I lived would I spend the rest of my life in a hospital quarantined from all that I knew and loved? What would happen to Sam if we all died? My exile under the stairwell felt endless, but as no additional bombs fell and no air raid sirens sounded, I was finally able to fall into an exhausted and anguished sleep with Sam quivering by my side.

In the meantime Marilyn, at the time of the explosion, had fled to the farthest corner of our acre lot, but not before she glimpsed backwards to make sure that Mother and Dad were alive and unhurt. At her last look, they were liberally covered with baked beans, grass clippings, and clay. Most of the neighbors, with Esther and Reuben in the lead, raced to the scene within seconds. Two members of the volunteer fire department chattered into their radios saying, "No, it's not a gas leak. Somebody just blew up something in their yard. No one is injured. The house and garage aren't damaged."

An hour or so later most of the neighbors finally left to continue their Saturday pursuits. Esther and Reuben, along with their three children, had stayed for the meal at my parents' invitation. Mother opened two cans of Campbell's baked beans to go with the ham, and Esther and Reuben concocted a green salad to which Esther contributed a cucumber and green pepper from her own back yard garden plot. The meal was almost ready when Mother noticed that Sam and I were missing and sent Marilyn to look for us.

Marilyn knew most of my hideouts and found me quickly.

"You're alive." I was in shocked ecstasy.

"Of course I am," she answered. "Why wouldn't I be?"

"I thought the Russians had come."

"The Russians didn't come. The neighbors came because the beans blew up."

She hauled Sam and me out of the sleeping bag and up the stairs. My humiliation was complete when she told Mother, Dad, and the entire Appleton family where I was and why.

Afterwards Mother once again lectured me.

"You're way too sensitive and gullible. You shouldn't be so upset over a loud noise and a little explosion. Nobody is going to die in a nuclear holocaust."

Mother had forgotten her own response to the fateful root beer explosion that occurred in Springfield when I was five and her ongoing anxiety about Bradford's deployment. She was as embarrassed by my obvious cowardice as she was by having created a talking point for all the neighbors.

On the complete mortification scale, Marilyn and Mother were front-runners. Marilyn was openly embarrassed, but, being solidly entrenched in her upbringing, never shared her feelings with anyone. Mother assigned blame to the heavy clay soil that trapped the steam and caused her beans to explode everywhere. She never did accept responsibility for our near annihilation. Dad remained stoic about the affair and shrugged off the amusement of the neighbors.

I remained part of two cultures, belonging to neither. Sam was a constant at my side.

To this day I have disliked sudden loud noises.

Neither Marilyn nor I have ever attended a clambake.

Chapter 12

FIRE!

Mother carefully flipped the page of our clipper ship calendar to December. That simple and beautiful act which charted the passing of our days hinted at this month being different from our previous two Ohio Decembers. For one thing, Bradford was scheduled to arrive home by mid-month. And Grace was planning to join us, flying into the Youngstown-Vienna Airport two days before Christmas. Although the sky had remained the depressing, monochromatic slate color characteristic of northeast Ohio from mid-November to late February, my heart was playing a joyful prelude that Monday morning.

The second thing that added to my joy was that I had permanently moved into Marilyn's room the weekend before Thanksgiving so Mother and Dad could paint the tiny bubble-gum pink bedroom a rather too minty shade of green. Mother thought that mint green would be a more suitable color for the grown-up son of the house.

Moving in with Marilyn was an upgrade for me, since her room was a very pretty shade of blue. Even so, the last thing Marilyn needed was a little sister crammed into a room that already contained two aquariums, a pair of little red-eared turtles, El Fago the cat, six or seven parakeets, and usually Sam. Fortunately, my personal belongings, other than my doll collection, were sparse and could mostly be housed in a small bureau in the tiny alcove that separated the three bedrooms. The doll collection was placed on the lower of the two shelves in Marilyn's closet. I'm sure that Marilyn longed for, and rightfully should have had, a room (or maybe a house) all her own to share with her menagerie. I give her lots of credit for her graciousness given that when Grace arrived over the holidays she too would be sharing Marilyn's ten-foot square bedroom.

We had been tweeted, gurgled, meowed, splashed, and barked awake by Marilyn's menagerie. After breakfast, Mother noted that the temperature was exceptionally cold even for the first day of December.

"Please," I begged, "it's so cold outside. May I wear my corduroy slacks to school?"

"No," Mother answered, "if you're cold, wear one of your new wool skirts and the blazer. Put on some tights. You'll be warm enough then."

Although recommended school attire for girls who were no longer in primary grades called for dresses or skirts and sweaters, when the weather was extremely cold, exceptions could be made. Mother had made two new wool skirts for me. One was plain green, and the other was a green plaid; both skirts went with my green blazer and proved warm enough to get me through most of the winter's cold spells. On this exceptionally bitter day I was hoping to apply the exception to the rule. I had always been most comfortable in the cold wearing corduroy slacks and sweaters, but Mother was not going to tolerate any argument from me about clothing.

Reluctantly, I put on the plain green skirt and matching blazer. Interestingly enough, I left for school that morning with my heart and footsteps light in spite of the no slacks ultimatum. I could hardly wait for Bradford to come home and for Grace to arrive for Christmas. The only thing that could have given me more joy would have been if Adela and Angus had planned to come for Christmas. That was not to be since they now were the proud parents of a new little girl.

The school day moved along. We had started to study geography that year, and I found I had a great liking for it especially since what we were learning about were places that I had seen during our summer camping trips. I arrived home that afternoon still upbeat and with a light heart. One less day to go before Bradford was home and Grace was in Ohio for the Christmas holiday!

Two and a half hours later, news of the events of that day would push me into a very adult world of horror and unthinkable tragedy.

Marilyn and I had finished helping Mother wash and dry the supper dishes, and I was lying on my bed reading when I heard the three long, beckoning beeps from the television that signaled some sort of emergency.

"We interrupt this regular broadcast with a news announcement out of Illinois. A Catholic elementary school in Chicago is the scene of a massive fire that started just prior to class dismissal for the day. Numerous injuries and some casualties are being reported."

I moved to the doorway of the bedroom, where I could see the television clearly.

"A five alarm fire is still burning at Our Lady of the Angels School near Humboldt Park. Many ambulances and other emergency vehicles are transporting injured children and nuns to area hospitals. Casualties appear to be mounting."

Mother and Dad looked up as I gasped and quickly turned to another station which was also airing news of the fire. Knowing my overactive imagination, Dad quickly responded, "Chicago is many miles away from here, and the school was probably old and in a very densely populated area. It can't happen here. You needn't worry about it."

He got up from the sofa and turned off the television. This action only triggered my anxiety and added a level of morbid curiosity.

The rest of the evening I spent ruminating over the fire. I wondered how many kids had been injured or killed. I worried about their families. I worried about my own school. Although Dad had told me fires like that couldn't happen in our community, I wondered if what he said was true. Parts of my elementary school had been built in the previous century. I wondered how old the school was in Chicago. How had the fire started?

Turning off the television didn't prevent me from hearing the radio or reading the afternoon newspapers. As the reports from Chicago began to circulate and the huge number of serious injuries and deaths mounted, I latched onto certain pieces of information. The school, like mine, was old and classes were large. I had often heard grumbling around our community about the size of the elementary school classes. The first of us baby boomers had overtaken the school population by storm, and thirty some odd kids per classroom was the norm.

Another piece of information was that the rooms in Our Lady of the Angels, just like my classroom, had doors with transoms, many of which were open.

Finally, the school had an English-style basement, and the top floor rooms looked over a black-topped parking lot on the south, north and west sides with concrete sidewalks on the east.

In addition to worrying about a nuclear holocaust, I became very fearful about my own school catching fire. My classroom was in the oldest part of the school and was also on the top floor. The windows were huge and hard to open, not that I had any inclination to jump out of them for any reason, but if a fire did occur, I was certain I'd be trapped.

Apparently I wasn't the only person who was a little worried about the school catching fire. The very next day the voice of our principal echoed throughout the building. Mr. Wheeler loved the new intercom system that allowed him to communicate directly with every classroom in the building or any individual classroom that he might select. He interrupted instruction at every opportunity, some days as often as every fifty or sixty minutes. Once I overheard my own teacher say, "We'd get more teaching done if we didn't have official interruptions during every class period."

On this day, however, he did have an important message for the entire school.

"The volunteer fire department will be conducting a series of fire drills throughout the next weeks. Any pupil who misbehaves during these drills will be sent to the office and severely disciplined."

This direct approach was designed to ease the fears of many parents in the community. Mother's and Dad's efforts to shield me from knowledge of the events in Chicago had failed. Although we were strongly discouraged from discussing the terrible events that occurred at Our Lady of the Angels while we were at home, all of us would be part of "blocked exit" fire drills during which we would practice alternative exits and pretend that one or more stairwells were impassable because of flames or smoke.

Not only did the firemen provide realistic scenarios, but they also staged one drill with a small smoke bomb to get us used to conditions in a real fire.

When the evacuation times from the building were not up to standard, Mr. Wheeler took to his intercom again. "May I have your attention, please. May I have your attention."

"Because of our school's poor performance during the last three fire drills, all students are to report to the auditorium for an assembly for corrective action."

Corrective action? Were we going to be punished for not responding quickly enough? I couldn't think of a single person in my classroom that had been goofing off or taking our fire drills lightly. Those kids whose parents had been most concerned had been told that whatever punishment the principal meted out for misbehavior would be doubled at home. My parents didn't say anything like that. They knew that I was already close to the limit of my emergency drill endurance. So far, in an effort to reassure parents, we had been given rides on fire trucks, promoted to junior fire marshals, provided with plastic fire helmets, exposed to flag drills, smoke drills, regular drills, window drills, air raid drills, and bomb threat drills.

The corrective action assembly consisted of an array of films shot during the height of the Chicago fire. Graphic pictures of this horrendous event were shown from the screen on the main stage to all students in grades 4-8. After the films, Mr. Wheeler lectured us at length about proper decorum and the importance of speed and smoothness during our fire drills.

The films were the first time that pictures of a terrible tragedy would be piped into my school and my consciousness, and while they didn't necessarily increase our speed as we exited the building, they did have a profound effect upon my own psyche.

I lost confidence in Dad's words of reassurance. After all, if such an event could never happen in our community, why did we have to watch such awful films and listen to the lecture afterwards and have regular timed fire drills with blocked exits and smoke bombs?

Over a period of time, the stories about the fire grew smaller and were moved to the interior pages of the newspapers. My anxieties about the fire, however, remained. Three years later a former student at the Our Lady of Angels School was discovered setting other fires and, when questioned, confessed to setting the fire that killed so many other children. I was relieved until I learned that the judge had not held him responsible. I attempted one final time to discuss this with Mother and Dad, but their only response was to encourage me to forget about it.

"You're too morbid," said Mother.

"Forget about it. It's in the past," said Dad. "You can't do anything about it."

The following year I entered high school and was profoundly grateful to be attending classes in an almost-new single story building. Our safety drills occurred only four or five times a year and were conducted without smoke bombs. My fear of being trapped in a burning building diminished.

When I started college, I felt extremely anxious about sitting through classes in the one hundred year old building that was in the center of the campus. After six weeks, I came to recognize that I feared being trapped in the upper story of that structure. Happily, most of my classes there lasted only an hour; my time there was limited. Halfway through my sophomore year, a new building was dedicated and, when finished, housed almost all of my classes.

The recognition of fire safety and exits remains a constant in my life. One of the first things my husband did for me after we purchased a one-hundred year old home was to build an emergency exit from our second floor bedroom.

Chapter 13
BRADFORD'S HOMECOMING

"I just wish he'd get here," exclaimed Mother.

Agitation and anxiety permeated her voice.

Bradford, having been honorably discharged from the army, was coming home.

He had been delayed in Germany by a baggage handlers' strike for what seemed like eons. Finally he had secured a flight on a military plane that carried him as far as Newfoundland. From there he had somehow been able to get to Summerfield and spent a night or two visiting with Angus, Adela and Grace.

For the entire month of November and the first part of December, Mother and Dad had been preparing for Bradford's homecoming. After I moved in with Marilyn, my little room was stripped of furniture, scrubbed, and painted. In place of my bed, chest, and dresser, Bradford's old bed, a small desk, an easy chair, and dresser had been arranged. Once these preparations were completed, Mother set about dusting, vacuuming, scrubbing, and washing until the entire house was a model of cleanliness.

She then proceeded to bake. Chocolate chip cookies, molasses cookies formulated from Grandma Harrington's secret recipe, sugar cookies, and Bradford's favorite mincemeat pie were among the first items. She planned meals for every day through the entire Christmas holiday. For all we knew, the entire U.S. Army was arriving home instead of one lone soldier.

Mother placed the telephone handset firmly in its cradle after hearing the latest itinerary.

"He's coming by Greyhound bus," she told Dad. "He should be in sometime tomorrow afternoon. Are you able to pick him up at the bus station?"

"Yes. Depending on when he gets in, I should be able to skip out of work for an hour to drive him home. I'll go back afterwards to finish out the day."

Even though Dad was just as eager as Mother to see his only son, he would never miss any more work than was absolutely necessary.

The reason he had to go for Bradford at all was because Mother didn't know how to drive, and she tended to move into full panic mode every time someone suggested she learn. In any event, Dad wasn't all that eager for her to learn either. I suspect he had visions of cars in ditches, frantic calls regarding flat tires, overheated radiators, minor scrapes with the police, and outright accidents. He willingly gave what time he had with his family, a not insignificant amount of his earnings, and even his socks to whichever kid needed them; however, he was always extremely reluctant to share his vehicle with any of us, including Mother.

This may have been because his first car, an old Ford Model A, had speed, power, and reliability unparalleled in Dad's universe. Once he purchased that Model A, he assiduously avoided most public transportation in favor of the freedom and the independence his private ride gave him. He became an undisputed king of the road, and though he was delighted to have any of us as passengers, he only very reluctantly allowed any of us to drive any of his cars. They were his: loved, cared for, appreciated, and unshared.

Unfortunately for Marilyn and me, the day that Bradford arrived home was a school day. Just as Dad would only leave work for the time required to transport Bradford to the house, Marilyn and I were firmly told that skipping school to welcome a brother home was not an option. Mother's rules regarding school attendance were unbending. The only reasons for missing school were high fevers, vomiting, or illnesses that resulted in quarantine. In spite of our pleas, we were sent off at the usual time to school. Mother was probably relieved not to have us underfoot as she eagerly anticipated the arrival of her long absent son. Besides, after an absence of three years, she wanted Bradford all to herself for at least one afternoon. With Dad back at work and Marilyn and me effectively out of the way, this desire was more easily fulfilled.

School was interminable that day.

Arithmetic was followed by spelling, which preceded reading, geography, penmanship, and science. Not even Mr. Wheeler's intercom interrupted the monotony, and for once, we had no fire drill. Up until that day, I was a relatively conscientious pupil who tried to pay attention and do what I was told, but for the first time I realized how easily I could dissociate myself from lessons unnoticed for short periods of time. While Mrs. Chapman droned on, I began flights into an alternate and earlier time during which every moment that I had shared with my brother and older sisters played through my head like the endless loop of a movie or a dream from which I did not want to wake up. I was in my own beautiful, pre-Christmas world of red, gold, green, silver, and blue lights.

The sweet and pleasant pungency of my beloved fir and birch trees in the Berkshire Hills replaced the workaday odors of chalk dust, eraser crumbs, and pencil shavings. Mrs. Chapman's voice explaining the different stages of the moon became a choir of angels singing Christmas carols to welcome my brother home.

Arithmetic was replaced by interstate bus schedules, spelling by the place names of the cities through which Bradford was now travelling, geography by the rivers he was crossing on his way home, and penmanship ovals by the names of each of my siblings.

I was fortunate that Mrs. Chapman, who had her hands full with thirty or so other kids, didn't notice my complete oblivion to any lesson she was trying to teach. Of course, someone might have informed her of what was going on in our household, but I sincerely doubt it.

How lucky I was that my flights of fancy were interrupted by flashes of connection just often enough to provide an occasional and mostly correct answer!

Finally, the hour for dismissal arrived.

I raced home to find my brother chaired at the kitchen table enjoying tea and a pile of molasses cookies. He wasn't, much to my disappointment, in uniform, but he was there. He was there in the flesh. He looked even thinner than I remember him and strangely older, with an occasional fine line around his eyes and mouth. He had Dad's eyes and Mother's beautiful mouth. He was sitting there; my symbol of perfection, my hero, my brother on the kitchen chair usually occupied by Dad.

Like an arrow flying to the bull's eye of a target, I flung myself at him and held on for life.

He was home!!

Mother, of course, was totally discomfited by my overwhelming emotional reaction.

"Now, now," she said. "That's enough of that. Let go of your brother and sit down or go play."

She would have preferred if I had responded with a subdued handshake or a quick peck on the cheek, but given the emotions that were raging within me, she and Bradford were both very lucky that my landing in Bradford's lap hadn't upset the chair and the kitchen table.

I was not going to be put off by the chilly Yankee decorum expected of a child not yet ten years old.

"When did you get here?" I asked him.

"About an hour and a half ago." he answered.

"Did you see Grace, Adela, and Angus?"

"Yes. They asked me to say hello."

"Is Grace still coming for Christmas?"

"Yes, I think so."

"Now that you're here, what are we going to do first?"

"Well," he answered, "after this week I'm going to be starting a new job."

"Oh."

I was vastly disappointed. I had innocently assumed that we would have until the end of the Christmas holidays just to play. In fact, I thought we'd play most of the time I wasn't in school.

Mother and Dad had different plans. As exciting and joyful as the occasion was, Bradford was an adult now and needed to become a wage-earner as quickly as possible. He was no longer the boy brother of my early childhood; he was serious about starting his career in business.

After a superb supper of pot roast and apple pie, we all sat quietly in the living room watching television. Bradford had already met Reuben and Esther Appleton, and Marilyn's entire menagerie. He became reacquainted with Sam, who had just been a puppy prior to his enlistment. He had already contacted one of the managers of the insurance company where he was going to work.

As the evening wound down toward bedtime, I felt, for the first time in my life, an appreciation of the wealth of family, life, and every Christmas I had ever known. Never again would the five of us live under the same roof, but when I went to bed that night, I knew that I was the richest kid in the universe.

I vowed then and there that no matter how far away from them I was, or they were from me, I would keep my three sisters and my brother in my heart forever. So far I've kept my vow.

Chapter 14
THE PIANO TUNER

The beautiful old upright piano that was permanently placed on the south wall of our living room in Ohio had been given to Mother by her Grandmother Thomas. Appearing miraculously on her birthday one cold January day, the piano stood in the parlor of the modest house in New Bedford where Grandma and Grandpa Jones, Mother's younger brother Henry, and Mother lived. The piano, a Jewett, was an extremely high quality instrument made up of a walnut case, a solid wooden soundboard, and all ivory and ebony keys. Forty years later the piano was showing signs of age, but Mother still kept it as carefully as she could.

Mother inherited her love of music from her own mother whose specialty was voice. Grandma Jones had a fine contralto voice and often was asked to perform at local churches and community events. With formal training she might have able to earn her living with her voice. Although Mother decidedly did not have Grandma's vocal abilities, she did have an excellent ear. Unfortunately, money for pianos and music lessons was in very short supply when Mother was growing up. Her father's career as a textile mill supervisor paralleled the vagaries of the national economy which was always up and down. In spite of this hardship, Mother progressed rapidly. She practiced assiduously, and after two years of lessons, she was a promising pianist. With more formal training, she too could have had a career as a musician.

Loving music as she did, Mother was eager for all of us girls to share her enjoyment. Grace, Adela, and Marilyn in turn had all taken piano lessons in Summerfield. Grace and Adela despised their teacher and, after a time, begged Mother to allow them to discontinue the lessons. After many heated battles, Mother finally gave in to their requests. Unlike her older sisters, Marilyn had progressed nicely until the time we left Summerfield for Ohio. Then, for lack of a teacher and Mother's inability to drive her into town for lessons, she had given up her lessons.

Although I had always enjoyed music in various forms, only when I reached fifth grade did I become passionate about learning to play an instrument. That year every fifth grade student received a small recorder called a Tonette. Under the tutelage of the music teacher, Mrs. Schwartz, we all learned some basic things about music including scales, intervals, simple triads, and staffs. After six weeks we had to surrender our Tonettes back to the school, but the seed that Mrs.Schwartz planted grew rapidly and bloomed.

I begged my mother for flute or clarinet lessons.

Mother said no.

She pointed out that she couldn't take me to music lessons because she didn't know how to drive, that flutes and clarinets cost a lot of money, and furthermore, we had a piano sitting in our very own living room that wasn't being used. Additionally, after a while my three older sisters had given up piano lessons: it seemed pointless to give any kid music lessons if all she was going to do was quit as soon as practice became difficult or boring.

I continued to beg, and Mother continued to refuse until one day she said, "If you really want to learn to play, maybe I can teach you."

Two lessons later, the wear and tear on the piano over the years had become painfully obvious. It had been in a flooded storage facility in downtown Providence, Rhode Island, during the hurricane that swept Long Island and New England in 1938, and it had suffered through at least one extreme heat wave which was evident by the blistered paint on the casing. The ivory was missing from at least one or two keys, and the soundboard, which had been cracked in the move to Ohio, produced a distinct buzz when certain notes were played. The felts on most of the hammers needed to be replaced, some strings were broken, and the entire instrument was pitched half a step flat.

Clearly help was needed.

Dad and Bradford were at their respective work, and Marilyn and I were at school the frigid and blustery day the piano tuner came. Therefore, this story isn't my own, but is my understanding of what happened as relayed at the supper table by Mother, who was both in anguish with embarrassment and amused by the event.

Sam had a rather un-Labrador tendency to become protective and argumentative when strangers were about and barked loudly as the tuner's vehicle pulled into the driveway. He growled at him before he could enter the house. Upon opening the door, Mother had to forcibly restrain this large, unhappy dog to allow the man to enter our house. By way of an apology and in true New England fashion, Mother made him a welcoming cup of hot tea and offered him a chair at the dining room table. She was delighted to see the piano tuner and wanted him to know how grateful she was.

Having been starved for company all winter, Mother had taken to engaging in lengthy, rather one-sided conversations with the milkman from the Claypool Sanitary Dairy, with the man who drove the delivery truck from the bakery, with the garbage collectors, and with the evening paper boy. As she sipped her tea, she informed the piano tuner not only of the forty year history of the piano, but also filled in details about our family history, the move to Ohio, Bradford's return from military service, and all the neighbors. Wondering when Mother might finally find the harbor and dock her conversational ship, the tuner arose and edged toward the piano.

Sam followed him.

"Hmm," he said as he carefully examined the exterior of the piano.

"As I was explaining to you about the heat wave," began Mother.

"Grrrr," Sam responded deep in his throat.

The piano tuner tried to ignore them both and opened his case of tuning forks and a second case that held felts, strings, hammer replacements, and key covers.

"PING!" He sounded the first tuning fork.

"Woof! Woof! Woof!" Sam barked.

"No!" said Mother firmly.

"Madam," said the piano tuner, "would you kindly remove the dog so I can hear better?"

Mother grabbed Sam by the collar, dragged him into our bedroom, and closed the door firmly. Sam, who was not happy at being prevented from doing his lawful duty as a guard dog, took exception and began to whine and scratch at the door.

"PING!" The piano tuner sounded a second note.

At this point, El Fago, the black kitten that Marilyn had recently adopted, emerged from his hiding place and pranced across the living room floor. El Fago and Sam, who had struck up a friendship of sorts, were united in their common desire to chase and devour all seven of Marilyn's parakeets that were housed in a large cage in the corner next to the piano. Today, deprived of his partner in crime, El Fago took matters into his own paws and began to climb up the birdcage about the time the third tuning fork emerged from its case on the floor.

Mother had learned over the course of several months to ignore Sam's and El Fago's forays towards the bird cage, although one of them, and we never were sure which one it was, had periodically been knocking over the cage. No birds had been injured; the only negative results were the feathers, bird seed, and water cups scattered over the carpet which needed to be vacuumed on a daily basis.

"SQUAWK!" Katrina, the first of the parakeets to live in the cage, and the leader of the flock, took exception to El Fago's appearance.

"SQUAWK! SCREECH! CHIRP!" All seven parakeets loudly informed the world that their space was being violated.

The piano tuner looked up. He himself looked enough like Jiminy Cricket to whet the appetite of all seven birds. He had large, dark, almond-shaped eyes, long eyelashes and furry brows, a little round bald head, a rather wide mouth, a chinless face, a pair of spindly little arms, and two skinny little legs. His pants were too short and his feet were too large. According to Mother, the only things lacking in the comparison were antennae growing from his head. In this regard I'd have to disagree with her: Jiminy Cricket didn't have antennae.

After fussing about the dog, the tuner was probably reluctant to complain about the cat and the parakeets. Thinking that she might help alleviate the man's frustration, Mother launched into another story about Katrina, the other parakeets, and Sam's reputation as a family guard dog.

The piano tuner continued in his attempts to do his job.

El Fago, meanwhile, having satisfied his parakeet-baiting urge, strolled out of the living room with his tail in the air and went to the linen closet near Mother's and Dad's room where he liked to nap under the bottom shelf. With both cat and dog out of sight, the birds began to show more interest in the piano tuner's forks.

PING! PING!

"SQUAWKKK! CHEEP! CHATTER!! CHIRP!!" All the birds sang.

I can only imagine the tuner's frustration as he carefully lifted another tuning fork from his case, sounded it, and tried to adjust another octave of the piano while Mother chatted, the dog scratched and growled, and the birds squawked ever more loudly.

Finally, the piano tuner spoke again. His voice was very stern.

"Madam," he said. "I simply cannot hear with all this racket. Will you please quiet all these animals!" He was desperate.

Mother thought out loud for a few minutes. "Perhaps I could cover the birds."

"Yes, yes, yes," panted the tuner. "That might work."

So mother went to the linen closet to retrieve the surplus army blankets we used for camping and routed El Fago from his hiding place. She threw the blankets over the bird cage not realizing that the cat had followed her back to the living room. As she had covered the bird cage, she also covered El Fago which caused him to erupt in wild yowls and the birds to react fearfully with their loudest squawking yet. Sam, who thought things that all good guard dogs thought, went wild trying to break out of the room to protect Mother from the strange man and the onslaught of birds.

Mother's solution had only added to the cacophony.

"I'm sure they'll all quiet down in a minute," said Mother. However, she sounded doubtful as she spoke.

At that moment, Marilyn came in from school. The piano tuner was quivering with frustration as Mother and Marilyn looked at each other while trying to contain their laughter.

Marilyn quietly removed the birds to her bedroom and ensconced herself with the entire menagerie...seven parakeets, El Fago the cat, Sam the dog, the fish, and the turtles.

The piano tuner was finally able to finish the job.

I don't know if the reason he never came back was because he was such an unwilling conversationalist and Mother wouldn't have him, if he was really all that terrified of the dog, or if El Fago in attempting to maul the cage full of budgies finally did him in.

Or maybe Dad just didn't want to have to pay his exorbitant fees.

"That's what they charge," said Mother reasonably when Dad complained about the cost.

"Combat pay," I heard Dad mutter under his breath.

The piano never was tuned again or worked on in any way until Mother and Dad prepared to move to Florida and shipped the piano to me. Randall, my husband, insisted that if we kept the piano, it needed to be restored to its former glory. We had the case refinished in a beautiful walnut, all the hammers, felts, and keys repaired, and the tuning completed.

The refurbisher suggested we leave the soundboard alone which we did. After several years, we gave the piano to Marilyn's oldest son Andrew for his two little daughters. Neither of his girls has expressed any interest in music, but he and his wife like keeping his grandmother's beloved piano in the family.

Chapter 15
COW GONE CRAZY

At the time of our move to Ohio, Dad was a metallurgist who worked in quality control. He was the link between his company's headquarters in Connecticut and the Ohio suppliers of raw materials and parts. Dad, who was enamored by most technologies, loved airplanes and airplane engines. He and I shared this passion and spent many happy and companionable Sunday afternoons watching planes take off and land at the local airport where a contingent of the U.S. Air Force Reserve was stationed. Mother, Marilyn, and Sam often joined us, but their enthusiasm for flight was far less than Dad's and mine. Dad taught me to recognize planes first by their profiles and then by the sound of their engines. As we watched the Air Force fleet land and take off, I could imagine flying those planes someday. Mostly the planes were Douglas C47s, but occasionally we would also see Fairchild 119s, the huge Flying Boxcars with the unique double tails. As we watched, Dad told me about all the different kinds of planes that were used to feed the people of Berlin during the Berlin Airlift after World War II.

"I'm getting bored watching the airfield," Mother said one stifling summer afternoon.

"Let's stay home for a change."

Although I was disappointed, I acknowledged that the sun was very bright and the temperatures were well into the eighties. Mother always did feel the heat, and I had a new Nancy Drew book waiting to be read.

The afternoon wore on. Mother had finally acquiesced to the

purchase of a large fan that year, and as long as Dad was home to deal with any electrical issues, she was content to sit in the living room with the fan aiding in air circulation while she read the Sunday papers. Marilyn was cleaning her aquariums and bird cages, and I was deep into my book. Bradford, who was working as an insurance agent, was busily running calculations at his desk.

Suddenly, I heard by father exclaim, "Come here, everyone! Look! See! A vee formation! Those are B52's!"

I rushed to the front door to see. How beautiful they were! All those planes heading to the local airfield! I moaned silently in longing and ecstasy.

Dad was modest to the point of diffidence about his work and rarely discussed it at home, but I could see the pride in his face as he watched the planes flying low overhead. He had helped perfect the engines in those B52 bombers.

"What are B52s doing here?" I asked.

"They're probably on a training mission," he responded. "Things are changing really quickly in the world, and the armed services have to keep on with their training to protect us. Dad knew my fertile imagination would run amok if he used the phrase "cold war" and had only reluctantly agreed to my wearing the school-issued dog-tags around my neck identifying my name, age, blood-type, and address because he thought it would bring me some peace of mind. We had been rehearsing duck-and-cover drills endlessly since I had entered the Claypool school system, and I was extremely conscious of the imminent nuclear holocaust looming over us.

Bradford appeared near the front door at that point and quickly affirmed Dad's comments. He then returned to his work, Marilyn went back to her fish and birds, and I resumed Nancy Drew. Nancy and Ned were among the few things that would take my mind from the realms of flight, bomb drills, and wars.

An hour or so later, Mother called to us, "Time for some exercise, girls. Bradford, do you want to join us?"

The evening croquet game was about to begin.

Dad and Mother had spent most of the first three Ohio summers clearing the back part of our acre lot. Originally our plot had been the back pasture of a dairy farm. The pasture had lain fallow for some years before a businessman had purchased the land to create a housing development. A significant number of brushy scrub plants, small trees, and grape vines had overtaken the pasture land which was, when we first moved in, infested with snakes and frogs. My parents had labored to the point of aching backs and blistered hands to produce a lawn worthy of croquet. We played every evening that summer unless rain or diminishing daylight prevented it. Sometimes Esther and Reuben Appleton joined the family, but more often just the four or five of us–depending on Bradford's schedule–would play.

Mother thought out-of-door play was good for Marilyn and me and encouraged us to make use of the cooler evening hours to get some fresh air. Bradford and Marilyn were ready that night for a rousing game of croquet, but I was an inveterate bookworm. I had to find out how Nancy escaped from the fur thieves who locked her in a cabin in Quebec. Besides, reading time in our active and often noisy household was always a rare commodity.

A third of the way through the croquet game - and just as Ned had burst into the freezing cabin to rescue Nancy, a boom like a gas explosion sounded overhead.

"I wonder what that was," I fretted.

We had finally overcome the bean pot episode, and none of us wanted to relive that day. Could it have been a bomb dropping?

I went to Bradford's room and looked out to the backyard.

"It's just a plane," called Dad. "That one was a fighter jet. He just broke the sound barrier. The noise you heard is called a sonic boom." I remembered learning about sonic booms in school and about how Chuck Yeager, a flying ace, had achieved Mach 1 in a plane he was flying. I wanted to see the plane, but it was long gone. Reassured, I returned to my book. At last I had reached the final chapters when Nancy, George, Bess, and their boyfriends were going to corner the thieves, recover the stolen furs, and return the money from the fake stock certificates to the unwary victims of River Heights.

Suddenly, I heard a screech of pure terror coming from the back yard.

Maybe Dad had been wrong, and a bomb had landed in the middle of the croquet court.

I raced back to Bradford's room and peered out of the window. The sight was beyond belief.

Mother was in full flight with croquet wickets wrapped around both ankles. She was brandishing her favorite blue-striped croquet mallet over her head like a lasso as she ran screaming towards the street. She was yelling so loudly and incoherently that all I could hear was something about a "goddamn cow." A Holstein heifer, also in full flight and shaking her head every few steps as she ran, followed Mother blindly.

Several feet behind the cow was Marilyn alternately hollering at the top of her lungs in apparent fear for Mother's life and laughing wildly as her feet flew in an attempt to rescue Mother. Dad brought up the rear waving his arms around and shouting at the cow, Mother, and Marilyn to stop.

Bradford, meanwhile, appeared to be struck dumb with amazement. He stood in the middle of the croquet court with his eyes and mouth wide open observing the scene.

Convulsing with laughter, I ran from Bradford's room back to the living room window to see how the chase might end. Surely either Mother or the cow would soon be winded enough that Marilyn, at least, would be able to catch them.

By this time, Leona and Delbert Woodson, who lived in the snug little yellow house across the street, were in their front yard watching the spectacle with their next-door neighbors, Rowan and Bubba Easton.

Leona was a tiny, hyperactive woman of uncertain age—she could have been anywhere from forty-five to sixty—from Kentucky. Even though she and Delbert had no children at home anymore, Leona lived to clean her house. From dewy morning to past sunset, she vacuumed, dusted, mopped, and scrubbed, and when she was finished, she'd start all over again. She spit-shined her yard every day too; even the scarce trees in our neighborhood had been trained not to let their leaves land on her lawn or gardens in autumn.

Delbert, who was from Tennessee, was far more relaxed. He

was perfectly happy being Leona Woodson's husband and, though a hard worker in his own right, was inclined every so often to take in a football or baseball game on the television and forego certain chores that Leona thought essential. Once, when a shingle had come loose from his and Leona's home, Leona asked him to check out the roof to see if any additional shingles were loose. Apparently, Delbert hadn't moved fast enough to suit her, for Leona dragged an extension ladder from their garage, propped it up against the house, and proceeded to the roof herself to check for damage.

For such a little woman, Leona had a very full voice. If hog-calling contests had been popular at that time, she would surely have been a champion. As the cow and human formation galloped toward her lawn and garden, she could see the inevitable result unfolding before her eyes.

"DELBERTT! DELLLBERRRT!!! THAT COW IS HEADING FOR MY FLOWERS!!!!!! DO SOMETHING!!!!!!

But there was nothing Delbert could do. Mother, the cow, Marilyn, Dad, and, by this time, the cow's owner had reached the prized lawn and flowerbeds. The chase continued with no one changing positions in the line-up but with a few add-ons after Dad and the cow's owner.

Through Woodson's yard, around the corner, and onto Hoffman Drive that heifer raced before finally, completely exhausted and trembling with fright, she stopped in Sansonetti's backyard, and the entire procession converged upon her. Mr. Walker, owner of the dairy farm just to the north, came up from the middle of what was by then a small throng of people.

"Darn noise," he muttered. "My cows won't even come in to be milked with that infernal racket.'

"That cow," shrieked my mother to Mr. Walker and the entire township, "is the spawn of Satan!"

Mrs. Woodson, who had recovered her poise, thought the plane that had caused the sonic boom was more likely the spawn of Satan and would not take settlement from Mr. Walker for the cow gone amok in her flowers. However, she scolded and harped on Delbert for the rest of the evening for not being able to stop the carnage on her lawn and in her flowerbeds.

Mr. Walker led the poor cow, dazed and dehydrated, home to the dairy farm.

After repeated reassurances from Mother that she was not hurt, and after untangling her from the croquet wickets, Dad escorted her and Marilyn home. Mother's sleep that night was broken by vivid dreams of farm animals on the rampage.

Having finally finished my book, I rejoined the family croquet game the following evening. Dad kept looking for fighter planes and B52s, Mother kept nervously glancing over her shoulders, and Marilyn and Bradford stole surreptitious glances at one another and giggled.

I won three out of three games that night.

Chapter 16
THE SHELTIES

While he was way beyond intelligent by human standards, Sam was untrainable. He was never easily or happily confined; he almost never came when he was called, and he did not heel, fetch, lie down, roll over, or do tricks. Although trustworthy with people, he was not averse to picking fights with other dogs. As a puppy, he chewed anything he could from old golf balls to Grace's best new suede pumps. He shredded Mother's stunning Martha Washington bedspread, pulled garbage from the bathroom and kitchen bins and scattered it over the entire house, ran away to chase cows whenever he could escape from us, and, at one point, managed to populate the entire neighborhood with a dozen black puppies who looked and acted just like him. Both Mother and Dad said that taking him camping with us was out of the question. Every summer when Mother, Dad, Marilyn, and I went on vacation, we left Sam at the Cloverhill Kennel.

In addition to providing boarding services for other people's dogs, the owners of the Cloverleaf Kennel, Mr. and Mrs. Johnson, bred and raised purebred Shetland Sheepdogs.

The first time we left Sam at the kennel and Marilyn saw these beautiful little dogs, she promptly fell in love with them. Their refined features, long coats, gentle manners, and willingness to do whatever their humans asked of them captivated both her and Mother. She began campaigning for another dog...one that she could train and take to dog shows and obedience trials like the Johnsons did with their dogs.

Upon returning from one of our annual three week vacations, Mother and Dad began to talk seriously with Marilyn about her desire.

"The house is already overcrowded with animals," said Mother. "You have guppies, gold fish, turtles, parakeets, java birds, canaries, a cat, and a dog. Last Christmas you brought home four guinea pigs from the science lab at school to take care of. We don't have room for any more animals."

As usual, Dad was more circumspect. "She already has an entire menagerie. What's one more animal?"

Mother sighed. Although she would never admit it, she too wanted a little sheltie.

"What are you willing to do to get this dog?" she asked Marilyn.

"Almost anything," Marilyn replied.

Soon a deal was struck. Mother's first priority (not necessarily Marilyn's) was to improve Marilyn's school performance. Convincing Marilyn to reduce her menagerie to manageable numbers was Mother's and Dad's second priority. After a series of negotiations, Marilyn agreed to achieve better marks in all her classes, find new homes for all the birds and most of the fish, give El Fago to a classmate who really wanted a kitten, and earn the money to pay for a Shetland Sheepdog puppy.

By Christmas Marilyn had done all that she was asked to do and had saved half of what was required to purchase the puppy. Mother and Dad, delighted with these improvements, provided her with the rest of the money needed. At that point in time, one of Cloverleaf's champions was expecting a litter, and Mrs. Johnson promised Marilyn first pick of the puppies. In due time the puppies arrived, and Marilyn selected the most promising of the four...a little tri-colored male who was registered with the American Kennel Club as Cloverleaf's Midnight Essence. Marilyn immediately dubbed him Shadow. When he came home on a cold day in late January, a champion entered our lives.

In two weeks he was totally housebroken. A month later Dad was taking Marilyn once a week to the local all-breed training club for lessons in training and handling her dog in preparation for showing.

A near-perfect team, Marilyn and Shadow were ready for their first sanctioned match in obedience late that March. That day in the ring, Marilyn's performance was flawless, and Shadow pranced through his exercises with the joi de vive of the champion that he was. They won their first ribbon with Dad and Mother proudly looking on and Mr. and Mrs. Johnson applauding loudly.

"This is a good thing," they all agreed.

Spring arrived late that year, but as soon as the back yard was free of snow, Marilyn created a training area, and she worked every day with Shadow. I hadn't seen her so happy since we came to Ohio. My heart sang for her success.

But I had also been bitten by the dog show bug.

"I wish I could have a sheltie too," I said.

"No," was the firm answer. "We can't afford another dog."

Mother was conflicted. She was delighted with Marilyn's progress and pleased that we finally had a family dog that was well-mannered, happy to stay in his own yard, and had no desire to chase other animals. But, Mother had just divested herself of one menagerie and now another one was looming on her horizon. Dad blanched outright. His eyes glazed at the thought of more vet bills, entry fees, dog food, and specialized equipment–not to mention the gasoline needed to drive to training sessions, clinics, and dog shows.

As Shadow and Marilyn became consistent winners on the show circuit, Dad, Mother, and I became regulars at the ringside. In a few more months, Shadow had won his first title, and Marilyn began training for the next one.

Meanwhile, I was becoming more and more discontented watching from the sidelines of the show rings. I wanted to train and show a champion and achieve recognition just like my sister was doing. My pleas for a dog of my own became louder and more frequent. With few opportunities to earn money and almost nothing with which to bargain, all I could do was hope and pray that someday my turn would come.

In the autumn of my eleventh year it did.

Mrs. Johnson telephoned Mother and Dad.

"I have an adult sheltie from a repeat breeding of two champions.

His older brother is on the AKC Register of Merit. I purchased this dog for my son William, but he isn't particularly interested in continuing to show dogs. I know that you've been thinking about a dog for your younger daughter. I'd be happy to transfer his papers to you at no cost just so the dog can have a good home."

This second to the last sentence was a complete misperception. The last thing Mother and Dad had been thinking about was adding another dog to the family. Mrs. Johnson was as good a sales agent as she was a breeder. This extra dog in her kennel was a liability, and she wanted him to find a home elsewhere.

The following Saturday, Wolverine's Happy Harold arrived in our kitchen. He was, according to Mother and Dad, our final dog. Harry, as he was called, was physically beautiful with an ideal sheltie double coat of mahogany sable, a full white ruff, and a narrow white stripe running from between his eyes to just before his nose. His temperament, however, was anything but happy. He was four years old, a middle-aged dog by most standards, and had behavioral issues common to shelties. Unlike Shadow, Harry had not been fully socialized as a puppy. He hated loud noises, a norm for many shelties. He was extremely shy around most people and exceptionally fearful of men.

The first step, according to Marilyn, Mother, and Dad, was to win him over with food. Mother usually cooked an extra egg for Sam each morning when she prepared Dad's breakfast–they all liked their eggs sunny side up. Soon she added extra rashers of bacon for Harry. Dad would hold Harry's bacon in his left hand while eating with his right. Harry was finally won over to Dad, and we soon began to work on helping him become comfortable with the rest of the family.

Harry eventually came to trust most of the household, and I joined the beginning obedience class with him at the local training club. I worked hard with him and began to imagine my first win. The spring show circuit loomed on the horizon.

Five months later Harry had learned to heel, sit, stand for examination, and stay upon command, but periodically he would flee the ring to the safety of his human family when a strange man approached, a sudden loud noise occurred, or unexpected movements threatened him. Harry and I finally graduated from our beginning obedience class with enough progress to warrant moving a step up.

After one or two sanction matches--small club-sponsored dog shows that gave owners and handlers a chance to acclimatize their dogs to the show ring without a lot of pressure to earn points for breeding, showmanship, or obedience performance—we entered Harry into his first American Kennel Club event.

In spite of his mediocre performance in all of the earlier venues we had tried, I persisted in my belief that not only had he made progress, which was decidedly true, but that he was going to place among the top four dogs, which was decidedly uncertain.

Having decided that purchasing a fast food lunch from the vendors at dog shows was both expensive and unhealthy, Mother spent a portion of her Saturday preparing a healthy lunch for the four of us to enjoy at Sunday's show. Meanwhile, Marilyn and I busied ourselves loading crates, water and food bowls, grooming equipment, leashes, and collars into the station wagon. We were both anticipating a good day on the morrow.

Sunday dawned remarkably sunny and spring-like, although the landscape remained winter-weary with snow melting everywhere creating large dirty puddles covered by cracked ice and exposing areas of muddy fields. The parking lot at the show venue was filled with potholes which grabbed at the wheels of the station-wagon and forced Dad to reclaim the correct direction every few minutes. He finally parked, and we began to unload.

With all of our equipment neatly stashed in the benching area of the show, and both shelties secured in their crates, Marilyn and I scanned the catalog for when our classes were scheduled. She and Shadow were in the Open A class which started at 10:30 that morning, and I was in Novice A later in the day.

Marilyn had done a creditable job preparing Shadow for his first Open class which consisted of off-leash work that included jumping over high and broad jumps on command, retrieving a dumb-bell, dropping on recall when commanded, and remaining in place both sitting and lying down for an extended period of time with the handler out of sight. Shadow did his best, and if memory serves me, he placed among the top four dogs.

I became very hopeful that Harry would do as well.

"Novice A class, next up," called one of the ring stewards.

I leashed Harry and walked confidently to the ring.

"Number 36, you're on deck," the steward said. He spoke quietly this time, because another dog and handler were in the ring.

They finished, and I entered the ring with Harry reluctantly at heel.

"Are you ready?" asked the judge. This was a standard courtesy posed to all handlers. It alerted everyone--dog, handler, stewards, and observers--that the judge was about to issue commands.

I nodded my assent, feeling very powerful.

"Forward," ordered the judge.

"Harry, heel," I said.

We started off at a brisk walk, with me holding the leash in my right hand waist high.

"Halt," commanded the judge.

I halted, but Harry, who was supposed to stop immediately when I did and sit squarely at my left side, continued on. He was frightened by the crowd and began to do an anxious "sheltie spin" circling around me and wrapping me up in the leash.

"Our first fault," I said to myself, "and it's a five-pointer."

I untangled myself and Harry.

"Forward," the judge ordered again.

We proceeded forward.

"Halt," the judge said.

This time Harry sat, but not squarely at my side. He parked directly in front of me, and rather than facing alertly forward, he gazed at my father. He was longing for his bacon treat. We had another five point fault.

"Forward," the judge said.

My sense is that the judge was not amused by our less than crisp performance.

I moved forward again, with Harry reluctantly at heel. When

we halted again, Harry did no better at sitting square than he had previously.

After what seemed an eternity, we moved from heeling at the normal walk, the quick walk/run and slow walk, to the figure eight.

The figure eight consisted of heeling around two ring stewards who were positioned between six and eight feet apart. The idea was to determine how well the dog and handler could stay together while weaving in and out of congested areas. In the middle of this maneuver, the judge called for a halt again.

Miraculously, Harry sat where and when he was supposed to. My confidence swelled again.

"Bring your dog to the center of the ring, please," was the next command.

No matter how poorly handlers and dogs performed, the judges were always courteous.

"Please, stand your dog for examination," the judge requested.

Harry wasn't about to let any strange man approach him, let along touch his head, back or legs. I had seen some dogs snap at a judge, but Harry was only interested in running away, which he attempted to do. The only thing keeping him in the ring was the leash.

Even in novice classes, the leash is considered a training tool and not a restraint. Running, or attempting to run, constituted a major disqualification.

Next came the recall exercise. This exercise required the handler to give a sit and stay command to the dog, to cross to the other side of the ring and there to wait for the judge who would then ask the handler to call the dog.

"Sit," I told Harry.

Harry sat.

"Stay," I told Harry.

Harry waited for a minute and then bolted from the ring.

Another disqualification.

To say I was disappointed would be an understatement. I can't say I was surprised, though. Harry just didn't have the ring presence, the joy, or the confidence that Shadow had.

I think I realized then that Harry probably never would be the happy champion in obedience competition that Shadow was.

After finishing our last two exercises and scoring less than half of the points required to win our first "leg" toward a title, I retreated to the station wagon for a little quiet time. Disappointed though I was, I was also determined that Harry and I would find a way to compete that would earn us some recognition.

Since my class was officially over and the winners announced, I decided to wander over to the confirmation rings where dogs were judged not on their obedience skills, but against their breed standards.

"Maybe we could compete in confirmation," I thought. After all, he actually had earned two confirmation points towards his championship in the "breed" ring when William Johnson owned him.

I posed this to Mother and Dad prior to our next sanction match.

They were skeptical, but they agreed that if we placed in the confirmation ring at a sanction match, we could try an AKC show.

Harry and I did win a ribbon at the sanction match. We placed fourth out of four. Not exactly a telling performance, but at least I had a ribbon.

Only as I was leaving the Shetland sheepdog judging did one of the ring stewards, whose duties had ended for the day, make a suggestion.

"Why don't you try junior showmanship?" she asked.

"What's junior showmanship?" I responded.

"It's a class specifically for kids," she answered. "You're judged only on your handling skills, not on the dog."

"Really?!"

To this day, I think I owe that anonymous steward my thanks.

"Thanks for the tip," I told her. "How do I sign up?"

She explained that all I needed to do was make sure that the dog I took into junior showmanship was entered in at least one other class, and that I showed up at ringside when junior showmanship was called.

Harry and I were good to go.

We took a ribbon in junior showmanship later that day.

From that point forward, we regularly entered one obedience class and then went into junior showmanship where we did reasonably well. Even so, Marilyn was always the better handler, and eventually, she offered to "finish" Harry in obedience, which she did. She also trained him to work in tandem with Shadow and began competing with them both in "brace." She won several best-in-show titles with both Shadow and the team.

I continued in junior showmanship and took into the ring with me at various points a Bedlington terrier, an Irish setter, a Pomeranian, an English bulldog, and German shepherd in addition to Harry.

Harry served one other very special purpose in the course of his life with us.

He sired a litter of puppies; one of those puppies became Mother's dog and constant companion.

Marilyn trained this dog as well, and this dog was every bit the champion that Harry could have been if we would have had him from puppyhood. We named her Harry's Autumn Breeze, and her name fit. She was a lovely little golden sable and had all Shadow's panache and Harry's beauty with a distinct feminine touch. Her call name was Windy, and she became Shadow's best friend. We all had great hopes for her.

Our hopes crashed when Windy was two years old. She was diagnosed with an incurable brain tumor, and after a day of non-stop seizures, we were forced to end her suffering.

Some people think that dogs don't have emotions like people, but we could all see Shadow grieving for his absent friend. He lost a little of the joy in his life that was reflected in his performance in the show ring. He was still outstanding but no longer had that indefinable "extra something" that marks a true champion. When Marilyn acquired her last sheltie six months later, another little female whom she called Bonnie, we all hoped that Shadow would recover some of his happiness.

He never did.

Mother, who repeatedly said she didn't want any more dogs in the house after Shadow and Sam, grieved for months.

She never did have another dog after little Windy.

Chapter 17

DELIRIUM

I felt perfectly well that cold Friday morning in mid-December. Although the temperatures were frigid, not much snow was on the ground and none was forecast. We had only three days of school scheduled the following week which was the week prior to our Christmas break. I was especially looking forward that Friday evening to participating in my Girl Scout Troop's annual caroling party. I could hardly wait for the school's annual Christmas concert which would take place the following Tuesday. Contrary to what Mother relayed later to the doctor, the county health nurse, her friends, and our family, no clue presented itself that morning regarding the serious turn my life would take within the next twenty-four hours. Accordingly, I remained in school for the full day, and after an early supper, Dad drove me to the gathering place where we would set off to carol in the small neighborhood that surrounded our leader's home.

I had a wonderful time and arrived home around 8:00 that evening.

"I'm very, very cold," I told Mother and Dad.

Shivering, I huddled over the heating vent by the sofa.

"You probably got chilled when you were out singing. Did you have your hat and mittens on?" murmured Mother. Her head emerged briefly from behind the evening paper.

"Yes, I did, but I'm really cold...shivering in fact. I can't get warm, and I've tried everything I can think of. And I feel so strange. My head aches and my bones hurt. I think I need to go to the hospital. Will you take me?"

"Hospital? That's absurd. There's nothing wrong with you that a hot bath and a cup of peppermint tea won't fix. Go soak in the tub for a bit and then fix some hot tea."

"I'll try, but I don't think anything will help," I asserted. "I think I'm very sick."

By the time I was born, Mother and Dad were experienced parents. They knew first-hand about measles, chicken pox, whooping cough and common colds. In spite of this, they tended to be taken by surprise with my tendency to contract not only the normal childhood illnesses, but also some rather exotic diseases. Not that they were insensitive, but they were remarkably naïve about certain things. My bout with the Asian flu was one of those memorable events. When I first became sick, their response was to try to treat the problem themselves using time-honored remedies such as onion poultices, home-made steam tents, and whisky and honey formulas. Only when the fever remained well over 101 degrees did they finally attempt to contact a doctor only to be told that physicians no longer made house calls and that we should go to the emergency room. Even then Dad didn't give up. A blizzard was raging outside and no way did he want to risk taking me to the emergency room. How he finally found a German doctor who was willing to brave the storm, I don't remember. The man spoke almost no English…he was a post-World War II refugee…but he was able to provide me with some relief on that occasion.

On the night in question, however, the hot bath followed by a cup of peppermint tea did nothing to warm me. I was freezing to the bone, my head felt strange, and my throat was extremely dry. Additionally, I was extremely nauseated and didn't think I could even keep the tea in my stomach.

"Let's call for an ambulance," I pleaded. "I feel like I'm dying."

This statement, though true, was interpreted by Mother and Dad as an unnecessary and extreme dramatization. They had heard enough.

"Stop whining and go to bed. We'll check your temperature after you're settled under the covers.

I tried one more tactic. Turning to Bradford I begged him to drive me to the hospital.

"I can't," he said, "Mother and Dad said no."

I dragged myself to bed. Marilyn, who was sympathetic, added two more blankets to the three I already had and cracked the window of our room. We always slept with the windows cracked open, even on the coldest winter nights, and even if we were sick. Mother believed the fresh air was good for us and that overheated rooms caused more illness than being in an occasional cold draft.

Snuggling down in the blankets with a hot water bottle at my feet, I waited for Mother to come in with the thermometer.

Pulling it from my mouth after the required three minutes, she checked it. Her eyes dilated; she shook the thermometer down and said, "I'll ask your father to check again just to be sure."

She put the thermometer back under my tongue and called Dad.

The second reading must have been the same as the first, for after he looked at it, he said, "Her temperature is 105 degrees. Is that what you read?"

"Yes," said Mother. "I wonder if she has pneumonia. Should we go to the hospital?"

"No," said Dad, "let's don't panic. We'll check again in the morning, and if it's still that high, we'll call the doctor."

After a fitful night, I woke up Saturday morning feeling worse. I was very thirsty but didn't think I could drink anything. I had no desire to get out of bed and mostly wanted to be left alone.

After the rest of the family had their breakfasts, Mother came in to check my temperature.

"How are you feeling?" she asked.

"As if I need to be in a hospital somewhere," I moaned.

She placed the thermometer under my tongue.

The gauge read 105.5 degrees.

Mother sighed. Dealing with a sick kid during the height of the pre-holiday season was not on her list of things to do that day. She told Dad that my fever had risen and that he should probably call a doctor. Calling the doctor, on the rare occasions when it needed to be done, was always Dad's job. After all, Mother reasoned, he was the one paying the bill.

Whether Dad had totally forgotten about doctors no longer making house calls, or whether he was stubbornly engaging in some magical thinking, I don't know for sure. I do know that he believed that if something should be a certain way, it would be that way. As a consequence, Dad was about to have another attitude adjustment at the hands of Dr. Yaroslav's receptionist. After conferring with the receptionist at the doctor's office for several minutes and trying to argue her into having the doctor stop by the house after his clinic hours, he scheduled an appointment.

"We have to take her to the office," he informed Mother.

He was somewhere between frustration at having to take time on a busy Saturday to take me to the doctor, humiliation at losing the argument, and growing concern over my obvious deterioration.

While he had been arguing with the receptionist, pain had set into every joint in my body. Every breath hurt, and I no longer was completely aware of my surroundings.

"I'm sorry," Dad said. He was sincerely contrite. "You'll have to get dressed so we can take you to the doctor."

I dragged myself out of bed and put some clothes on.

As soon as we reached the doctor's office, the nurse, bless her heart, beckoned us in to his office. As she was going through the preliminary process of weighing me and recording my symptoms, she said, "Your Mother told us that you didn't tell her you were sick so you could go to school yesterday and to a party last night. Why didn't you tell her you weren't feeling well and ask to stay home?"

"I felt fine yesterday morning," I insisted. "I didn't feel sick until I got home last night."

"Hmm," she responded.

I know she was suspicious about the onset of this disease. She took my temperature, did a throat swab, and called in the doctor.

He reviewed the chart, performed a short exam, and came up with a diagnosis.

"You have scarlet fever," he said. "Do you know what scarlet fever is?"

I didn't know, and frankly I didn't care. I knew I was very sick.

"Scarlet fever is highly contagious," he went on. "You and all the people you live with will need to start taking antibiotics immediately, and you will be placed in quarantine by the county health department. That means that you will not be allowed to leave the house for at least three weeks, and only those people who need to go to work or do necessary errands will be able to leave. If your fever keeps going up, you might have complications."

"I need to be in the hospital," I answered.

The doctor demurred. He turned to my father and said, "Are you or your wife able to do the required care? She's very dehydrated and will need constant monitoring. If she doesn't start taking in fluids and eating a little..."

He left his sentence unfinished.

"I think we can handle it," answered Dad.

He remembered seeing Grace, Bradford, and Adela through whooping cough, and the entire gamut of measles, mumps, chicken pox, Marilyn's various bumps and bruises, my Asian flu, and Mother's bout of phlebitis.

"Okay, then," answered the doctor. "We'll start with the antibiotics. She'll need to soak in a tub of the hottest water she can handle for at least a half hour, and then give fluids...as much as she can take in. Ginger ale, Seven-up, tea, water, and either popsicles or Jell-O should help."

Dad took me home with the doctor's orders written on a notepad. Mother began making Jell-O and tea.

Family plans for the Christmas holiday were ruined. Bradford wanted to invite a woman he was dating for Christmas dinner, but that was out of the question. Mother and Dad had hoped to attend a church supper prior to the holiday and decided not to go even though Mother was desperate to get out of the house for an evening. I would not be attending school the half-week prior to our break and that meant no Christmas concert for me. I was devastated.

Marilyn, however, was ecstatic. Because she was not "employed outside the home" and was still considered a minor school-age child, she too would be housebound. Her job, Mother informed her, was to help take care of me.

I didn't want to be taken care of. I wanted to stay in bed and be left alone until I recovered, got sent to the hospital, or died.

For the better part of the following week the fever raged in spite of the antibiotics, the hot baths, the fluids, and the soft diet. The pain increased until I could visualize myself being consumed by the pathogens rampaging in my body, erupting into flames, and reducing my body to a pile of ashes. In between these paroxysms, I thought about Christmas. Even though I was almost twelve, I wanted a Betsy McCall doll with both a skating skirt and a horseback riding habit. I dreamed of fire and Betsy McCall dolls intermittently until the day when the disease gained control. Exhausted by fever and spent with pain, my mind left my body in bed and went to another place.

It is one of only two times in my life when I experienced a complete dissociation.

It was beautiful.

I laughed out loud with the joy of it and clapped my hands appreciatively as each firework sounded and grew in the heavens and then burst and disappeared. It was like attending a Fourth of July fireworks display and a symphony concert all at once. Skyrockets and fireworks of multiple colors went off around me, brilliant reds, cobalt blues, the deepest of greens, and the brightest of yellows flew past my eyes and swirled around and around me. Music erupted from deep in the ocean and enveloped me in a rich symphony filled with violins and trumpets and textured with cellos, basses, tympani, and oboes. I could hear each individual instrument and see every color, and yet, they all blended together to create such a masterpiece of art and music as to defy any attempt at a full description. I united with the show of colors and music and became the explosions and the instruments and all the colors of the universe.

Wherever this place was, I wanted to stay forever.

I don't really know how long I remained in this glory, but when I returned and found myself still in bed, I was sweating as if I had run a marathon. My sheets were soaking wet, and Marilyn was looking at me curiously.

She was laughing too.

"You're hallucinating," she said. "You're laughing your head off."

"I think the fever broke. I'm going to go take a bath."

While I soaked again in the tub, Mother put clean sheets on the bed. It was two days before Christmas Eve.

"The doctor said you could help decorate the Christmas tree if you're up to it," Mother said.

I didn't quite have the energy to engage in holiday preparations, but I went into the living room anyway and put a few ornaments on the tree. I was exhausted by the fourth one.

"I need to go back to bed," I said. "I feel really weak."

The following night, Dad brought in a pile of gifts that he had purchased for Mother. Marilyn and I helped him wrap them and placed them under the tree.

Each day after that, I tried, at Mother's and Marilyn's urging, to stay out of bed a little longer until finally on Christmas I was able to remain up for most of the day.

I received my Betsy McCall doll with her two outfits.

I wasn't able to quite complete all my schoolwork, but I didn't fall too far behind owing to the fact that my absence occurred prior to a holiday, and mostly, the class was reviewing the work of the previous fifteen weeks.

The bout with scarlet fever was the last serious illness to trouble me until the summer before my senior year in college. That summer I contracted a severe case of shingles, but Mother and Dad had learned a valuable lesson and encouraged me to see a physician as soon as the symptoms appeared. The early intervention resulted in minimal scarring, a complete recovery, and no serious after effects. Mother's and Dad's philosophy regarding fresh air and the treatment of childhood illnesses has stood the test of time. The trend to over treat such ailments with antibiotics nowadays, resulting in antibiotic resistance, has never been an issue in our family, and I have never been hospitalized for more than six hours.

Chapter 18

THE PILOT AND HIS NAVIGATOR

Throughout the 1950s and 1960s, our travels often consisted of crossing Pennsylvania and New York to go to Massachusetts. "Going back East," we called these events, and other than an occasional foray into Michigan and Wisconsin, Mother and Dad took us to Massachusetts to reconnect with our sisters, brothers-in-law, and the growing number of children that were part of our family before we journeyed to some other area of New York or New England. I always anticipated these trips with mixed feelings. I cherished the time with my two older sisters and their families, but travelling with Mother and Dad to reach Massachusetts posed some challenging issues.

We had no Garmins or Siris or any other global positioning devices or mobile phones that told Dad what he needed to know to get us where we were going, so Mother assigned herself the task of planning the route, navigating, and map-reading.

In spite of her illusion of being in complete control, her navigational skills were marginal at best.

For one thing, she didn't always understand the conventions of map reading. Often she became lost in the translation between what the map was telling her and what she was trying to tell Dad. For her left was right and right was left and north was sometimes down and south was anywhere. This lack of spatial ability caused no end of disputes between Mother and Dad, and it often resulted in wrong turns, missed directional signs, plenty of tears, and outright tantrums as Mother insisted she was right, and Dad (more or less) tried to follow her directions.

Discussions regarding map folding were also frequently heated. Dad refolded his maps as neatly as if they were new after Mother arranged them so she could easily find her place. Doing this caused Mother to lose her place, further compromising her ability to discern where we were and where we might be going.

Then again, she had never learned to drive and consequently didn't understand the many things that would have been helpful to Dad such as giving him advance notice when he needed to transition smoothly into another lane or exit or enter a highway. She didn't know how to read road signs correctly which led to occasional "near misses" with other cars and the considerable annoyance of their drivers as Dad tried to negotiate several lanes of traffic at once while she yelled orders at him.

Other than the yelling, Dad never was too concerned with the results of poor map reading and navigation. Sometimes I think he deliberately lost himself while driving so he could see more of the country. This tendency, along with his unwillingness to stop and ask for directions, resulted in constant back-tracking and generally inefficient time management as far as Mother was concerned. It led to frequent and heated conflict because, for Mother, trip perfection consisted not only of setting up and breaking camp in timed, close-order drill, but also in minimizing the number of times we had to turn around and travel the direction from which we had just driven for the past hour. While Mother loved to travel, it took her many years to relax enough to believe that the journey was as much fun as the destination.

I might have been ten years old and on one of these trips when I first became aware of Mother's and Dad's particular version of marital politics. After three or four years of driving the full length of the New York Thruway, a highway that was continuously under construction and never finished, Dad was growing tired of the speed, the amount of traffic, and the on-going road rebuilding.

"Let's take another route when we go back East this year," he suggested to Mother that April as they began to plan our summer trip.

"It will take a little longer, but if we leave on Saturday morning we, can drive halfway across New York and stop at one of the state parks in the Finger Lakes area. What do you think?"

Marilyn and I weren't excited when we heard the phrase, "It will take a little longer." We were strictly on the page of arriving in Massachusetts as quickly as possible to maximize time with the family. We weren't asked for our opinion, however, and Mother embraced the idea of avoiding the New York Thruway.

"I'll write to New York and get information about what state parks are available in the area around Syracuse," she agreed, "and we can choose a park after we hear from the Department of Tourism."

What Mother found out was that either Cayuga State Park on Cayuga Lake or Watkins Glen State Park on Seneca Lake would work. A further conversation ended with a decision that we would spend the weekend at Watkins Glen even though driving to the south end of Seneca Lake would take longer.

"We can pick up U.S. Route 20 in Buffalo and follow it all the way to Seneca Lake and then drive south on Route 14 to get to Watkins Glen. If we stay there over the weekend and then drive on to Summerfield, we'll arrive rested," she said.

On the last Friday in July, we loaded up the car, and early on Saturday morning we headed for the Finger Lakes.

Dad drove, and, as usual, Mother attempted to navigate. Things had gone remarkably smoothly until we reached Avon, New York.

"Thurston," she said, "You missed a turn back there. We're on Route 5."

Dad, accustomed to Mother's infinite capacity to get confused any time we had to deviate from a straight road, sighed. "Where does the map indicate we should be?" he asked.

"We should be on Route 20," answered Mother, "but we're not. We're headed south."

"According to the map, Route 20 takes a bit of a southern jog here," Dad answered.

"No it doesn't. We're on Route 5." Mother's voice increased a few decibels.

And so the conversation went, with Mother's tortured voice continuing to rise in volume until, with relief, Marilyn saw a sign that indicated we were still on Route 20 and also on Route 5.

Mother had a difficult time believing she was wrong. This posture was one of her more endearing and aggravating qualities.

"Well," she said, "you must have corrected yourself when we turned right and then left back there."

"I'm just reading the signs," Dad answered.

"And I'm just reading the map," Mother snarled back.

This conversation went on the better part of the forenoon and lasted until we saw a sign that indicated a little public park was a mile ahead. Mother's watch read 11:15 a.m. Even though we were only two hours from our destination, Mother and Dad both wanted to stop. Mother wanted to eat, and Dad, who was never much interested in food, wanted a break from driving and listening to directions.

Having lunch promptly at 11:30 was an inflexible part of Mother's itinerary. Wherever we were, whether it was along a scenic coast, a parking space in a major metropolitan area, or a roadside picnic table in the country, we stopped at 11:15 for our lunch. She almost always packed a picnic lunch. She and Dad believed that stopping at fast food eateries wasn't as healthy as a home-made lunch. Besides, feeding a family of four even at a hamburger stand would have cost extra. One time Mother and Dad actually stopped in Hartford, Connecticut, and had lunch on the lawn of the state capital. It was 11:15 a.m., and even though Adela's and Angus's house was a scant thirty minutes away, lunch had to be eaten at 11:30.

Years later I have to acknowledge that Mother and Dad were right to veto fast food except as an occasional treat.

As we turned out of the park after our meal, Dad, for whatever reason, turned left.

"Where are you going?" Mother barked at him.

"Back onto Route 20," Dad answered. "We want to go east to get to the park."

"But you're not going east," Mother informed him. "You're going west."

"No. I'm following the sun." Dad answered. He was decided in his opinion.

"Well, the sun sets in the west," Mother told him.

"Yes, it always has and probably always will."

I'm still surprised Mother did not completely blow up at this last pronouncement.

"So why are we going west?"

"We're not. We're going east." Dad was growing impatient.

"Well, it's afternoon, and the sun is beginning to move west from its noon position. If you're following the sun, you're going west."

Dad looked up at the sun, and then over at Mother.

He had, on this occasion, been bested and turned the car around.

Dad was at fault more than once. I recall the day we were floundering around the lower peninsula of Michigan looking for a short cut to Ludington State Park. We finally arrived after Dad abandoned the short-cut and took the more conventional route to the park. Only after we had set up camp and settled around the fireplace did I observe Dad rather surreptitiously refolding his map. I happened to look at the date on the front, and it was five years older than I was.

Mother saw this too.

"No wonder I couldn't locate the road from this map," she said. "When this map was printed, the road hadn't even been built."

Again, she was right, and Dad had to eat a large piece of humble pie.

Dad liked to play the odds. I suspect that in his younger years he was a good poker player, although neither my Grandma Harrington nor Mother approved of gambling. I do know for a fact that both Dad's brothers liked to "play the ponies" and dropped several pennies competing with each other at cribbage.

Dad's gambling took a unique turn when he began to track the mileage of his cars. Initially, this was a required part of his expense accounting for work, but how far he could go on one tank of gas became a game with him.

He never stopped for a fill-up until his calculations indicated he had less than two miles worth of gas. We were back on the New York Thruway and driving east once again one blistering summer day when Dad announced proudly, "We have thirty miles to the next service plaza which should lower the amount of gas in our tank to less than a mile. I'll stop for gas there, and you girls can get out and stretch your legs if you want."

I wasn't sure I wanted to stretch my legs if doing so required me to leave the car. Air-conditioning in cars, now a standard feature, was a luxury of only very wealthy people in the 1950s. If I couldn't be in a lake cooling off, the next best thing was riding in the back seat of a car with the windows down.

Two miles from the service area, the car began to sputter and slowly lost power. Dad was able to pull to the relative safety of the broad shoulder of the road before the engine died.

We were out of gas.

Mother said nothing. The temperature was ninety or more degrees; we were hot, thirsty, and stiff from riding and couldn't leave the confines of the car.

Fortunately for us, the New York Thruway had a program in place where the state troopers carried two gallons of gasoline in their vehicles to give to motorists like Dad who had miscalculated their mileage.

Unfortunately for us, we had to wait a half hour for a state trooper to appear.

"Are you folks having car trouble?" he asked politely when he arrived.

"Um, not exactly trouble." Dad blushed. "We…um…ran out of gas."

The trooper apologized. "I normally carry two gallons in my cruiser, but I just gave it to another fella a few miles back. I'll either send someone else or come back to you. I might be a while, though."

An hour later we were on our way to the service area. The rest of the day both Mother and Dad were unusually quiet.

The following year we were again driving east on the New York Thruway. Mother had located the next rest area so we could stop and prepare lunch (the time was 11:15).

"We'll be stopping soon," she announced. "Are you hungry?"

She had just finished her question when the inevitable occurred. The car began its slow deceleration and Dad drifted to the side of the road.

"Engine trouble," he murmured quietly after a quick glance at the gas gauge.

"Wait here," he told the rest of us as he cautiously exited the car, "while I check things out."

He lifted the hood and pulled out the dipstick from the crankcase.

Mother slid over in her seat and peered at the gas gauge.

"You're not fooling anyone tinkering around under the hood," she said when Dad returned to his seat. "We're out of gas again."

Marilyn and I remained silent.

This time the state trooper arrived on the scene fairly quickly. After he left Dad said, "I just don't understand why we don't get the same mileage on our trips that we get in Ohio. I had the mileage factored to within a tenth of a gallon."

Mother looked murderous.

Twelve months later we were once more on the New York Thruway heading east when shortly before our 11:15 a.m. stop the car lost power, and Dad maneuvered it to the right side of the road. By now, we had learned by heart the painful scenes of this particular movie and the accompanying emotions which followed each scene. Mother's frustration, Dad's confusion and embarrassment, and our own discomfort played out in the usual script.

Once again a state trooper located us. The difference was that this year state troopers were no longer carrying cans of gasoline to assist stranded motorists. Perhaps the officials had recognized the inherent dangers of carrying gasoline in the trunk of cruisers on hot days, or perhaps the troopers themselves had decided that their responses to drivers who didn't check their gauges regularly was overly compassionate and enabled irresponsible behavior.

In any event, this particular trooper seemed to take a pretty dim view of our situation, and he definitely didn't have any gasoline to spare. He informed Dad that he could either call for a tow truck to bring us some gasoline, or we could wait for a good Samaritan-type driver to take Dad to the next service area to buy a gas can and bring some gasoline back to the car.

I could've sworn this man was the same trooper who had helped us out the year before.

Anyway, Dad didn't like either of the options. Putting himself at the mercy of strangers who might have all kinds of motives wasn't appealing to him, and a tow truck would've cost extra. After carefully thinking through the matter, he determined that he had just enough white gas to carry us to the next full-service area. We normally used the white gas to fuel the Coleman camping stove, but in an emergency, it could be used to propel the car as well.

Dad emptied all the white gas we had into the car's tank, and we were on our way. I noticed that he kept the fingers on his left hand crossed the entire distance and wiped the perspiration from his forehead while he shelled out his money to the service station attendant. He was so relieved that he actually provided a generous gratuity to the teenager who then offered to clean the windshield.

Mother finally broke her silence. "Really, Thurston? Three years in a row…really?!?"After we set up camp that afternoon, I noticed Dad sitting at the picnic table with a pen and notebook. He was scratching his head over a long column of figures. Finally, he looked up.

"I know where I went wrong," he said.

"Oh?" responded Mother.

"Yes."

Dad was almost smug.

"When I calculate the mileage per gallon of gasoline the car has nobody in it but me, and I'm driving in a relatively flat area. On our trips, the car is fully loaded with all our camping gear, our clothing, and three more people, and we're driving up and down some hills. No wonder I keep running out of gas. Our mileage just isn't as good."

Mother was beyond comment.

One Sunday years later, Dad almost ran out of gasoline again. We were deep in the eastern Adirondacks and the only open gas station could not accommodate the camping trailer and pick-up truck that replaced the umbrella tent and station wagon.

Mother and I gave him the benefit of the doubt that time.

Chapter 19
LAKE GEORGE

"Where do you want to go on our vacation next summer?" Mother asked.

As Marilyn and I grew older, Mother and Dad included us more often in trip planning.

She and I didn't miss a beat.

"Lake George and Rogers' Rock," we answered.

Mother and Dad weren't always unschooled in the ways and minds of kids...asking for our vacation preferences not only meant more cooperation from Marilyn and me, but also eliminated any tendencies towards complaining.

"After all," Mother reasoned, "if they make the final choice, they'll be happier living with the consequences."

Six months later we began our yearly trek east to Massachusetts. After a week of visiting with the Summerfield branch of the family, we headed north and west to the Adirondack Mountains of Upstate New York.

Like a long, narrow sapphire, Lake George nestles in a bowl of Canadian Shield rock east of the High Peaks of Adirondack Park and south and slightly west of Lake Champlain into which it drains by way of the LaChute River. The lake itself is thirty-two miles long, two hundred and fifty feet deep in some places, and three miles at its widest.

The mountains surrounding it have stood sentinel for many thousands of years. They are covered with dense forests of mixed deciduous and evergreen trees. A closer inspection also reveals numerous rocky outcroppings of granite. The dark green forests hint at a certain gentleness and refinement of character, but they are still dangerous to the uninformed and arrogant. Winter snows and wind blowing from the north and west can bind residents in place for many days. Climbers and hikers become lost, chilled, and disoriented. In some areas the lives of endangered timber rattlesnakes take precedence over human needs. In the summer, thunder booming and echoing across the rocky slopes creates an illusion of a storm three times its actual size.

On May 31, 1791, Thomas Jefferson said, "Lake George is without comparison, the most beautiful water I ever saw; formed by a contour of mountains into a basin...finely interspersed with islands, its water limpid as crystals, and the mountainsides covered with rich groves... down to the water-edge: here and there precipices of rock checker the scene and save it from monotony."

Even Jefferson's words don't do the place justice.

Designed and partially built by the Civilian Conservation Core in the 1930s and completed after World War II, Roger's Rock State Park on the north end of Lake George had 332 tent sites. Each site was three times again the size of most of the other places where we had camped, and significant boundaries of trees between the sites created privacy shields and muffled the sounds of other campers. All the sites had stone and concrete fireplaces carefully constructed to allow outdoor cooking.

"Do you think we can find a campsite on the lake shore?"

This question started the annual ritual. Selecting the campsite was always first, for in the late 1950s and early 1960s reservations for camping in a state park were unheard of. Whenever possible we selected one of the sites that abutted the lake even if we had to wait one or two nights in the designated overflow area which was an open field. In 1958 the park was a popular place, and after our first stop there the previous year, Mother and Dad learned that to obtain one of the preferred sites we should arrive on Sundays as close to noon as possible.

"You arrived at a good time," the park ranger at the camping office said. "Three families just checked out and all of them vacated lakeside sites. Do you know which one you want or do you want to check them out first?"

Marilyn and I knew which one we'd prefer, but Mother and Dad wanted to evaluate their options before making a final decision.

"We'd like to look first," Mother said.

"That's fine," answered the ranger, "but as soon as you decide, come back here so we don't assign the site to someone else."I noticed that two or three other cars had joined the queue waiting to check into the park. No doubt the ranger was hoping for a quick selection so the people in the cars behind us could also register.

We drove to the three sites, and Mother and Dad immediately decided on the same place that Marilyn and I had chosen. While Mother put lunch on the picnic table with my help, Marilyn walked the shelties, and Dad drove back to the office to make our selection official.

After we had eaten, Mother and Dad chose the place to pitch their tent. Each of us reported to our assigned corner of the tent and together pulled the floor taut, placing one tent peg near the corner for Dad to pound into the earth with the back of his axe-head. Then, while Dad put the center pole in place, Marilyn and I blew up the air-mattresses.

Mother's job was to put the camping cots together and place them in the tent, followed by the air-mattresses, sleeping bags, knapsacks of clothing, extra blankets for each cot, and finally the pillows.

After Mother's and Dad's sleeping quarters were arranged, Marilyn unfolded the dogs' crates and positioned them in a shady area. As she completed settling the dogs, I hung the curtains that Mother had made for the station wagon and made up the beds in the station wagon where Marilyn and I slept with the dogs. While Marilyn filled the five-gallon plastic water containers, Dad cleaned the ashes from the fireplace and neatly stacked enough wood to last us for two or three nights. Meanwhile, Mother and I organized her camp kitchen.

"I'm going to check out the lake for minnows," said Marilyn.

She loved to take a small, aquarium-sized fish net and capture minnows. She also liked to troll for plant life, but the lake didn't support many fish or plants, though she was successful at collecting a small school of minnows for study.

"I'm going to take a break and read the morning paper," said Mother. She moved to her lounge chair by the fireplace. Mother was more relaxed at Lake George than at any other place I can remember. She had no household issues to worry her, no kitchen appliances that ran on electricity and caused anxiety, and no phone calls from irate farmers regarding cow-chasing retrievers.

"This is the life," Dad murmured. He was appreciative of the peace and quiet after the long drive east and a week of visiting with his older daughters and their growing families. Other than periodically having to replenish our supply of firewood or white gas for the cooking stove, Dad also could relax. He was free from the ongoing stresses of work, and because the rest of us were so calm and content, he had no family issues to resolve, no one else's anxieties to relieve, no place he had to go, and no reason to rush to get there even if he did.

The place invited us to be at peace, each soul separate and unbegrudging of others' rights to be separate as well. Marilyn could wade into the lake and catch minnows and collect samples of the few water plants that grew near the shore without Mother's criticism that she engage in pursuits more fitting a teenage girl. Here I could read as much as I wanted to without constantly being nagged to complete a job or being told that I was somehow in the way of what others wanted to do. Marilyn and I could walk the dogs without scrutiny from neighbors, for many people brought their family pets with them to the park.

Evenings at Rogers' Rock brought wood smoke, the smell of cooking steaks and hamburgers, flannel shirts, and company around the campfire. Earlier that day, we had become acquainted with a Dutch family from Amsterdam. The youngest of their children was my age. She almost always stayed near her parents and two older siblings because she was the only one who spoke unbroken English, and her skills as a translator helped her family converse. Her father worked for the United Nations, and she and her older siblings attended the United Nations school. Mother and Dad had invited them to share our campfire. My parents talked for a long time with these people, whose last name has faded from my memory. However, I clearly remember them discussing the role of the United Nations in the aftermath of World War II and the reconstruction of Western Europe.

We all went to bed at ten; like most campgrounds, enforced quiet hours began at ten and lasted until seven the next day.

"Shall we go for a quick swim before breakfast?" Mother asked us as soon as we were up the next morning. Because of our shore access, we had a private beach, and even though the park officials did not endorse swimming from this little cove, they did not outright forbid our doing so. Every morning we would swim. Flying in the face of Ohio conventions at the time (something at which she excelled), Mother believed that early morning swimming was good for us. She believed it served to wake us up thoroughly and helped develop strong constitutions. She always joined Marilyn and me in this pre-breakfast exercise while Dad started the fire and fried eggs and bacon. I loved swimming in Lake George! We gamboled liked a pod of whales for thirty minutes or more before wrapping ourselves in towels and heading to the fireplace to warm ourselves prior to sitting down for breakfast. The lure of the opposite shore of the lake appealed to me, but a three-mile open water swim was beyond my eleven year-old capability. I vowed to become a strong enough swimmer to reach that far shore one day.

"Look at that!" I heard Dad exclaim the third night around the campfire.

"At what?" Mother, Marilyn, and I queried.

"There, on the horizon." Dad was animated.We all looked then as he pointed to the northwest sky.

The Northern Lights had exploded into a vivid display of unearthly beauty. They blossomed like the color spectrum I had only seen in my science textbook. For the better part of twenty minutes, violet, blue, green, yellow, orange, and red arced and flashed over the tops of the mountains and disappeared as quickly as they arrived followed by more and greater brilliance.

Days in our paradise on Lake George flew by swiftly like

multicolored gems sliding from a broken necklace. Some days were rubies, as if the fiery passions of my mother expanded and then dissipated into nothing. On those days, my joy was a continual symphony, crisp and cleanly knifing through me with exquisite pain. Other days were more like the calm, deep green emerald that was my father's nature and could be found in the trees' reflections on the water. We had yellow days in the sun hiking around Fort Defiance and Fort Mount Hope. We explored the vast Fort Ticonderoga which was located ten miles north of us on Lake Champlain. We had blue afternoons, too, which we spent on the beach or swimming in the water.

One day as I sat on a rock by the shore, I paused from my reading to look eastward over the lake. I wondered why our family was so much at peace here but not so much so at other places or other times. I wondered what the magic was that enabled us to be so emotionally close. Perhaps, I mused, not worrying about the trappings or possessions of suburban life slowed us down and gave us more time to think before we had to engage in anything. Maybe less of everything we thought we needed was better than having to take care of too much.

"I'm living on borrowed time," Dad used to say, "and I'm having the time of my life."

As I repeat these words to myself, they weave themselves in and out of my heart like the colorful stretchy loops I used as a child to make potholders on the small hand loom I received one year as a Christmas present. The memories of my summer weeks on Lake George flood my senses. I can enjoy once more the smell of freshly perking coffee, and the aroma of frying bacon, potatoes, and onions over a wood-burning campfire on a cold morning. I will always savor the memory of spending an entire day on a granite outcropping overlooking Lake George and reading a book. I can cherish the cold water and exhilaration of an early morning swim.

Mother and Dad didn't know any mental health experts, but they did believe that investing in experiences was far more important than investing in material possessions and that travel provided an education equal to anything we might learn in school. Our summer and weekend camping trips were the greatest gift they gave me, and of all the places we visited during our travels, the time we spent at Lake George remains imbedded in my heart as the set-point for learning to be in the moment.

I know now that I grew up privileged beyond any common measure.

I'm living on borrowed time, and I'm having the time of my life.

Chapter 20
GRACE AND LOUIS

"What would you like to drink, Mary? We have wine, beer, or Manhattans."

Louis, always hospitable, was ever eager to help Mother mellow out before she could disapprove of anything or anyone. He was also ready to assist Dad in quenching his thirst after a long drive. Louis had set up a drink tray on the front porch before he fired up the barbecue on the back end of the driveway.

Late that August afternoon, we had arrived in Summerfield and had gone directly to Grace's house for dinner. Grace, Louis, Adela, and Angus always shared entertaining responsibilities when Mother, Dad, Marilyn, and I travelled east to see the family. Grace and Louis had offered to put some chicken on the grill while Adela and Angus accompanied one of their children to a baseball game.

Although Grace's marriage to Louis in June of 1962 was one of the bright spots of that spring and summer, Bradford, Marilyn, and I did not attend the wedding.

Bradford was working, and Marilyn, newly graduated from high school, had received an invitation to serve as an apprentice and helper to a professional dog handler who was driving to Florida to campaign her three dogs on the Florida show circuit. Hortense Tennenbaum was a prominent member of the local all-breed training club. Although Marilyn wanted to go to Grace's wedding, she also was eager to explore professional dog handling as a career. This opportunity was just too good for her to pass up.

Without Marilyn, I didn't want to go either.

For one thing, as I grew into adolescence, the clothes that I had worn during elementary school began not only to appear a little shopworn and dated, but they also no longer fit my changing body. Throughout sixth and seventh grade, I had repeatedly asked for some new school clothing on every special occasion...first for Christmas, then for my birthday, and finally for Easter.

"We can't afford new clothes. Your old ones will do just fine," I was told.

So when Grace's wedding came, I didn't have anything to wear, and I was fairly certain Mother couldn't afford anything new for me. I didn't want to go to a wedding wearing the same yellow flowered dress that I'd been wearing for two and a half years and that old pair of scuffed saddle shoes.

The second reason I didn't want to go was because I didn't think I could handle the full blast of Mother's conflicted feelings about the wedding. The six hundred mile plus distance between Ohio and Massachusetts once again made communication difficult. Grace had included Mother and Dad as much as she could in her wedding planning, but logistics prevailed, and many decisions were necessarily made without Mother's input. This resulted in Mother once again having to come to terms with her lack of control over her three older children. Keenly perceptive, I knew that all her control issues would be directed at me now that Marilyn was leaving the nest in the same time-frame as Grace's marriage.

Miraculously, perhaps because Mother, and maybe Dad, thought that it would be easier to travel directly to Massachusetts with no kids in tow, they agreed to my remaining at home. Therefore, the only things I know about the wedding are that it was held at St. Laurens Catholic Church in downtown Summerfield, that some of the service was in French, that Grace looked beautiful in her tea-length dress, that Mother's shoes pinched unmercifully, and that Mother had tripped over one of the kneelers as she entered her pew just prior to the beginning of the ceremony. All of these things I learned piecemeal from looking at pictures, listening to other people's conversations, and asking questions.

A year later, I was sitting on the shady front porch of the house on Monroe Avenue, enjoying a tall glass of birch beer, a much favored treat that was unavailable in Ohio in the early sixties. Resting there, I contemplated the good fortune that had befallen our entire family, especially Grace, when Louis became my second brother-in-law.

"...and then, the night of the reception, the hall burned to the ground."

I checked back into the conversation just as the story ended. The hall where Grace and Louis had their reception burned? I wondered who was responsible.

"What on earth happened?" Mother asked.

I could tell she was worried that somehow Grace and Louis might be held responsible.

"We think the caterers dumped hot ashes from one of the trays into the garbage."

"So who paid for the damage?" Dad asked, cutting right to the chase.

"The caterers were held responsible. We really didn't know anything about it until we returned from our honeymoon," Grace answered.

"Anyway, the hall was insured," Louis said, "but we don't know if they're going to rebuild it or not."

I drifted away from the conversation again to the quietude of my corner on the porch. Not every family was lucky enough to have as good a mixologist as Louis was, I mused. In particular, he made excellent Manhattans. This I learned from listening to his cousins who were there to welcome us and share the meal. I had also learned from my unabashed eavesdropping in the corner that Louis's mother and one of his cousins had helped Grace clean, paint, and decorate the first floor of the duplex that she and Louis had rented to start their life together. The result was lovely. Grace had chosen a soft, warm peach color for her walls with light green and gold accents. The few pieces of furniture she and Louis purchased were French Provincial in style and provided a subtle reference to Louis's ancestry.

Louis's family was French Canadian. His parents and a handful of other relatives had emigrated from Quebec to the United States many years before. They had left a large contingent of the Thibidoux clan in Trois Rivieres, but visits back and forth over the border were common. In the course of Louis's lifetime, I never met all of his family, but I immediately liked those that I did know.

Louis himself had an expansive personality, filled with bonne homme, laughter, a wide practical knowledge of world affairs and politics, and an appreciation for a good party. He and Grace were generous hosts on all occasions. Louis had found his place in the world, embraced it, and was one of those rare individuals...an entirely happy man, comfortable in his own skin.

Within the Harrington family, Louis's slap-stick brand of humor became legendary. No topic was sacred, and all of us in turn were the unsuspecting straight-men to his jokes. His four brothers-in-law served as particularly good targets.

None of them, however, were the wonderful targets that our cousin Jeanne and her husband John were. Jeanne and Grace were the oldest of the girl cousins in the extended Harrington family. They had been especially close since childhood, and Jeanne was like another sister as far as Grace was concerned. As we grew older, many of the rest of the cousins drifted apart, but Jeanne, like the five of us siblings, stayed close to the family fold. When Jeanne married John McKenzie and Grace married Louis, the twosome became a foursome. One of this foursome's best known escapades happened on a fall day.

"I'd like to see the Norman Rockwell Museum," Jeanne said.

She and John had driven from South Dartmouth to spend the weekend with Grace and Louis.

"That might be fun," responded Grace.

Louis and John agreed to the trip, and the four of them set off for Stockbridge and the home and museum of Norman Rockwell.

The drive through the Berkshire Hills is always magnificent, but the day they chose to go was made to order: crisp, cold air, a faint odor of wood smoke, and the tang of a fine apple harvest permeating the air. Jeanne, Grace, and Louis enjoyed the brilliance of the October-blue sky and of the orange and red leaves tumbling in the wind, but John was somewhat immune to these latter experiences. A rapidly progressing case of macular degeneration had left him blind.

Arriving in Stockbridge, the four of them decided to eat lunch at the Red Lion Inn before proceeding to the museum. Grace was fond of the quiche served there, and she and Louis wanted a martini to fortify themselves for the trip through the museum.

At the museum, Louis took the lead.

"We'd like tickets for three adults, please," he said.

The ticket seller, a sharp-eyed Yankee, said to him, "I count four of you."

"Yes," Louis said, "but we only need three tickets."

"Why is that?" asked the seller.

"Well, you see this man here?" responded Louis.

"Yes, of course," responded the woman. A longish line was forming behind Louis, and she was beginning to be a bit impatient.

"Well," said Louis, "he's blind. You can hardly charge a blind man the full price of a museum ticket when he's not going to look at any of the art."

"How extraordinary!" replied the woman. She had gone from mild irritation at the hold-up to complete befuddlement.

Although I wasn't present for this particular adventure, I can imagine the woman looking over her bifocals at Louis and John.

"It hardly seems fair," Louis went on, "to make him pay when he can't really enjoy the show."

"I'll have to check with the manager of the gallery," she said. "We've really never encountered this kind of request before."

John, meanwhile, wasn't about to be outgunned by Louis. He spoke up for his own cause and pointed out that he was only along for the ride and pleasure of the rest of the family.

"I won't use any of this artwork," he promised the ticket-seller.

The manager duly appeared when summoned, and Louis, now supported by John, repeated his request.

Grace and Jeanne went to hide in the ladies' room.

I honestly don't know if Louis really thought he could make a case for John or if he was just pushing the boundaries of humor by poking gentle fun at a somewhat hidebound ticket-seller or by even poking fun at John himself. But whatever the motivation was, both the manager and ticket taker began to come over to "blind men can't see the art or have much use for it, so why should they be charged" side of the issue.

After a brief conference, both the ticket-seller and manager agreed that John should be allowed to enter the museum at no cost.

I never tired of hearing this great story!

After five years in their rented duplex and shortly after the youngest of their three children were born, Louis and Grace had saved enough money to buy a small Cape Cod style house in North Summerfield. This house, though farther away from the old neighborhood, was just as charming as the duplex on Monroe Avenue had been.

The annual New Year's open house at this Thibidoux residence became another legend in the family. Everyone Louis and Grace knew was invited, and the throng grew so thick that there was standing room only. Even if the conditions were truly polar, the party became an indoor/outdoor event. Some years close to a hundred people were invited, and almost everyone who was invited chose to come.

Louis was always good for a cold Manhattan, a good laugh, a story, a joke.

One of the bitter ironies of Grace's life with him was that Louis's funeral was held on the 43rd anniversary of their wedding day in St. Laurens Catholic Church...the same church where he and Grace had been married. It was the last event to take place there before the church was torn down. A portion of the service was appropriately conducted in French.

The funeral crowd was so large that the Summerfield police department had to send officers to deal with the parking situation. The funeral procession that crossed the Connecticut River to St. Anthony's Cemetery was so long it closed the main bridge in downtown Summerfield.

I think Louis would have enjoyed working the crowd that day.

When he left us, something fine and beautiful passed out of this world forever, leaving us richer in memories but poorer because of his absence.

Chapter 21
THE CUBAN MISSILE CRISIS

"Looks like the Russians are up to something," Dad announced after the Huntley-Brinkley report that night in early October.

The relationship between the Soviet Union and the United States of America was rapidly reaching a new boiling point in the autumn of my thirteenth year, and as tensions increased so did Mother's and Dad's anxieties. On this occasion, the Central Intelligence Agency had discovered, through photo reconnaissance, some curious structures being built on the island nation of Cuba. Various government agencies thought these might be missile silos under construction and increased their fly-overs to verify what was happening.

"I hope we don't go to war," Mother said.

She had been saying this after almost every evening newscast since the failed Bay of Pigs invasion had embarrassed the United States eighteen months prior to this news report.

Perhaps if Mother and Dad knew that I had become an avid listener, if not viewer, of the Huntley-Brinkley report, they might have been a bit more circumspect in their own viewing habits as well as in their evening conversations. They were, as I have explained earlier, notably unaware of what I might be seeing, hearing, thinking, feeling, or planning to do. I have no doubt that they assumed I was still young enough to be blissfully oblivious to world events.

They couldn't have been more wrong.

I had started listening to Chet Huntley and David Brinkley a year earlier because I was riveted by the strains of Beethoven's Ninth Symphony which ended their nightly newscasts. At first I paid little attention to the news itself, but I found myself listening to more and more of it to insure that I wouldn't miss the ending credits and the music.

I couldn't help but be aware of the gravity of the Cold War as I waited faithfully every night for the beauty and force of Beethoven's music. Meanwhile, in direct counterpoint to the timeless power of the music, the news grew steadily worse.

"When the Russians attack us, will Ohio be one of the first targets?" I asked Dad one night at supper. I was anxiously aware that the land area around the Great Lakes was a major steel producing and manufacturing center. I wanted to sound as casual as possible, hoping that no one would realize I had been listening to the evening news. As fearful as I was of the pending nuclear holocaust, I didn't want to lose access to Beethoven. I knew that my parents would deal with my fears by changing the channel.

"The Russians aren't going to attack us," Dad answered. He was deep into his pot roast and gravy. "But if they did," he added, "no one will be safe."

His words increased my anxiety ten-fold. Even so, I was still able to function tolerably well enough to get through most days. I functioned well, that is, until the superintendent of the school district decided to prepare all of us kids for the crisis that everyone thought was coming.

In accordance with a request from public safety officials, he made sure that the signs marking our school basement as an air-raid shelter were in all the correct locations and clear from any defacing graffiti that might confuse an uneducated public. And he ordered a series of air-raid drills in each building.

When my classmates and I were younger, our duck and cover air-raid drills consisted of us diving under our school desks when the fire-alarm bells rang one long and two short blasts in succession. As little third and fourth grade students, none of us were rocket scientists, but we weren't completely witless, either. We knew that no air raid drill was going to protect us from the results of advanced nuclear weaponry. Now that we were eighth graders, we were bigger and taller. No longer could we hide handily under our desks. The school officials grappled to find a solution. Finally, we were ordered to clear out all superfluous items from our school lockers so we could jump into them instead of hiding under our desks.

I'm not really sure how jumping in and out of our lockers would save us from a nuclear attack any more than scrambling under our desks, but I did feel more secure at the thought of hunkering down in the locker I shared with a classmate. In any event, the drills soon began.

They proceeded much the same as always--one long blast on the fire alarm bells followed by two short blasts, then another long blast and two short blasts until every kid was tucked neatly into his or her locker. But a problem emerged. The school was so crowded that two kids had to share a locker. Since two normal-sized eighth grade kids couldn't exactly fit into one locker, one kid was supposed to jump into the locker; the other kid was supposed to close the door and lean into it covering his/her head with both hands.

This system created more of a disaster than the one it was attempting to avert. Understandably, some confusion existed about which kid jumped into the locker and which one stayed outside. Two kids may have jumped into the same locker and gotten stuck. I could easily imagine this happening if they both jumped at the same time. Apparently, the school officials either found this to be a problem or thought it could be, for after our first drill, the procedure changed and all kids were ordered into the hallway facing the lockers, with heads covered and eyes closed.

On October 14th, seven months and two days after my thirteenth birthday, the bottom fell out of my world.

A U-2 spy plane had taken pictures clearly showing sites where nuclear ballistic missile bases were under construction in Cuba. Eight days later, on October 22nd the crisis reached a flashpoint. On that day, not only did President Kennedy order a blockade of Cuba, but he also sent a letter to Soviet Premier Nikita Krushchev demanding that the completed missile bases, and those still being built, be dismantled and all nuclear weapons be returned to the Soviet Union. An attack on Cuba became more likely.

"Things are getting more serious by the minute," I heard Mother and Dad say.

"What's DEFCON? Are we going to war?" I asked them.

"It's possible," Dad answered. He ignored my question about the meaning DEFCON.

I escalated from profound anxiety into full-blown terror. I couldn't eat and didn't sleep well and lived every moment in dread as I waited to hear the announcement that the United States was launching an attack on Cuba, thereby starting World War III. I retreated deep into myself wishing there was some way, any way at all, that I could prevent this. The on-going discussions at school, the constant updating of news, and my own perceptions of the unfolding world events created a living hell. During the day, I put one foot in front of the other, going through the motions of being a typical kid. Evenings I spent listening to the news, hoping and praying that I would awaken the next day and the threat of war would be over.

Years later a friend said, "Eighth-graders are like first-graders on hormones. They have undeveloped cerebral cortices; they're unfocused, and they live in the here and now."

That certainly could have been said of me as an eighth grader, but with modification. I probably did have an underdeveloped cerebral cortex, but I was certainly focused and couldn't wait to leave the here and now and transport myself to a happier and more peaceful place free from the on-going threat of annihilation. I was thinking like an adult and responding to my own thoughts like a child.

In the vernacular of the time, I was a basket case.

"This day," Chet Huntley intoned, "Premier Nikita Krushchev has ordered the Soviet ships carrying missiles bound for Cuba to proceed in direct defiance of President Kennedy's mandate. If the ships continue on course, they will be in Cuba tomorrow. The President and Joint Chiefs of Staff have raised the military readiness of our armed forces to DEFCON 2."

The date was October 24th.

That was the day my childhood ended.

I knew that I was going to die by the end of the week.

Two more days passed, and Mother was listening to the Winifred Barry show when a radio announcer came on the air.

"We interrupt this show with an important development out of Washington," he said.

"Earlier today at least one of the missile-bearing Soviet ships sailing to Cuba appeared to turn around and is heading eastward away from the U.S. ships that have blockaded Cuba. We have also heard from an unofficial source that intense negotiations between President Kennedy and Soviet Premier Nikita Krushchev are underway and that a tentative agreement has been reached to avoid a nuclear showdown. Please, stay tuned as further developments are imminent. We now return to our regular program."

After two more days living in a nightmare of fear and uncertainty, the negotiations paid off: the crisis ceased. My prayers were answered! No war! Finally, the world leaders had come to their senses and compromised! I don't know if the entire world breathed a palpable sigh of relief, but I know I did. I wasn't going to die after all. I could, I thought, return to a more normal and kid-like existence.

That didn't happen though. The threat had ended, albeit temporarily, but my childhood never returned.

Somewhere in the span of time between October 14th and the easing of what history later labelled The Cuban Missile Crisis, I had been launched by world events into a warped kind of late adolescence with adult-like concerns and issues. I became introspective and even more bookish, and I gave up the kites and hopscotch that had given me much joy four months earlier. I no longer wanted to play. I had been given a second chance at life. With this chance an important goal became paramount. I needed to decide what kind of person I wanted to become and what kind of life-work I wanted to prepare for. I didn't have any more time to waste; another crisis would come, maybe soon. I felt profoundly depressed that I had no special skill or talent that seemed worthy to develop. I didn't have Grace's self-discipline, or Bradford's brains, or Adela's joi de vivre, or Marilyn's athleticism. I had some talent musically, perhaps, but the likelihood that I could develop that in any way seemed to me to be slim or non-existent, and besides, music was always more a form of relaxation than it was a potential career. That left only dogs and school, and since Marilyn cornered the dog show circuit, school became my option.

I would, I decided, excel at my studies and try to become a physician before I died. Although I wasn't crazy about math, I liked science, especially biology and chemistry. I also knew that at that time, kids majoring in science at college received a lot more financial assistance than kids majoring in anything else. I might even receive a scholarship to help fund my own education!

I began to work much harder at school. I knew I was in for many years of rigorous study and began to like the challenge of preparing for the innumerable exams that were part of my anticipated college preparatory courses. Even if I didn't manage medicine as a career, I hoped to achieve some other success academically.

After October 1962, I rarely went to school dances. Dancing, dating, boys, and having a social life weren't all that important anymore. I had left all that behind with no regrets. My new life became books and studies; my social life was limited to my involvement in the high school pep club, choir, and the Future Teachers of America.

Fifty-five years later I remember the gripping fear of being thirteen and powerless to change or even influence world events. Now, however, I have the vantage point of knowing that I was not alone during those difficult days. I'm certain that in the fall of 1962, a youngster of thirteen years or so, growing up in the former Soviet Union, was just as afraid as I was.

This knowledge gives me hope.

My wish is that all the leaders of the world would remember what it is like to be young, powerless, and afraid.

Chapter 22
SAM'S NIGHT ON
THE TOWN

Snow arrived in mid-October that year, presaging a winter that even by New England standards was exceptionally bitter. The shelties' double coat grew luxuriantly thick, and Sam's fur gained a Labrador sheen that bespoke extra oils to protect him from the elements. The wind and cold were relentless. Mother had hot tea and scones ready to ward off the chill when I arrived home from school every afternoon. On Saturday evenings, she roasted potatoes to go with the meatloaf. Chicken stew became a regular feature in our weekly menu. Dad's commute around northeast Ohio grew challenging. He was frequently late coming home owing to road conditions, and Mother worried incessantly about traffic accidents.

Winter storm warnings were non-existent in 1962, but no National Weather Service updates were necessary to inform us that a blizzard was raging outside that evening in early December. Several inches of snow had already fallen, and drifts were piling up around both the house and the garage doors. The wind was at gale force and blowing incessantly, and the pressure reading on Dad's barometer was rapidly dropping. Close to 9:30, Marilyn and I were both ready to go to bed.

"Come on boys," she said to all three dogs. "It's time to go out."

Normally, she would have grabbed Sam's collar prior to opening the back door, but on this occasion, whether she was in a hurry to get the dogs out and back inside because of the cold, or whether she just grew careless, I don't know. But however it happened, Sam was not secured prior to the back door being opened, and he flew into the moonless and frigid night with Shadow and Harry close behind him.

"No! Noo!! NOOO!!!" Marilyn yelled.

"Now what?" Mother questioned.

Mother, being tired from her household chores that day and already depressed by the unending gray and white landscape of the northern Ohio winter, was more irritable than usual.

"All three dogs just took off into the blue!" cried Marilyn.

"How did that happen?" Mother and Dad asked simultaneously.

"When I opened the door, Sam ran right through it before I could grab him, and Shadow and Harry followed!" Marilyn explained.

"You'd just better hope they don't get as far as Tuscarawas Avenue," declared Mother, "or they're as good as gone."

Mother's assessment was correct. Tuscarawas Avenue was also an Ohio state route, a major north and south highway preferred by many over-the-road truckers as a connection between the New York Thruway and the Ohio Turnpike. We were all justified in our anxiety. Sam was all black and Shadow mostly so, while Harry was a dark sable. No driver would see them in enough time to stop even if that were possible on the snow-covered and slippery highway.

"We'd better go look for them," sighed Dad.

He shed his bathrobe, threw on a pair of pants, an overcoat, and his galoshes and went to the garage. Marilyn, having quickly dressed, followed him and began to call all three dogs by name. I wanted to go too, but Mother forbade my joining them. Even though Dad was driving at a snail's pace and the only conceivable bad outcome for Marilyn and him could be driving the station wagon into a ditch, Mother was worried because the streets were barely passable, and she couldn't see the advantage of one more person being out in the height of the storm. She and I stayed behind in the hope that one or more of the dogs might return home.

"We'll start on our own street," Dad told Marilyn, "and if we don't find them, we'll go over to Rachel Avenue."

Rachel Avenue, like Leah and Elliot Avenues, ran north and south. All three streets included many houses that Sam had visited in his previous escapes and were just east of the many dairy farms that so often had been unwilling hosts to our errant dog.

Dad drove and Marilyn called repeatedly as they drove north and then south on Elliot, Rachel, and Leah Avenues. They were unsuccessful and widened their search to include the other streets in our allotment...Hoffman Drive and Eugene Street. Marilyn was more and more frantic at the loss of Shadow. Dad's exasperation at Sam's ability to pick the worst possible time to escape grew exponentially. Both he and Marilyn grew colder and more anxious as the storm worsened and the minutes passed.

Meanwhile, Mother, Bradford, and I remained in the warmth and relative comfort of our house. Periodically one of us would go to the front door and call one or more of the dogs by name and then withdraw to the living room to warm up before trying again.

Twenty minutes had passed when Bradford announced, "I hear one of the dogs."

A sharp bark...unmistakably sheltie-sounding...announced the arrival of not one, but both shelties. In spite of their thick winter coats, both dogs were shivering. We called them into the house and waited for Marilyn and Dad to appear with a chastened Sam in tow.

"Now," Mother said, "if only your father and Marilyn would come home." Her voice quavered with fear and fatigue.

Her wish was granted soon after. Turning into the driveway, Dad gunned the engine of the station wagon, cleared two drifts in the middle of the driveway, and landed Marilyn and himself safely in the garage.

"Not a paw print or a bark," Marilyn announced. She was inconsolable.

Just then a swirl of Shetland Sheepdogs with wagging tails and happy barks surrounded her. Shadow and Harry were safe at home! Marilyn and Mother breathed collective sighs of relief.

Sam was still missing.

"We can't look anymore tonight," Dad said. "Tomorrow will come early enough, and we all need some sleep."

"But what about Sam?" Mother asked.

"He'll be able to take care of himself," Dad answered. "Any dog that's fool enough to take off in the middle of a storm like this deserves what he gets. He'll be home by morning; you can depend upon it."

"What we can depend on," Mother countered, "are phone calls from all the neighbors, especially if he's out chasing cows again."

"The cows should all be in tonight," Dad said. "No farmer in his right mind would leave livestock out in the fields in this kind of weather."

Marilyn cracked the windows in our little bedroom, and I cuddled down under a weight of blankets. I fell asleep promptly, smug in the knowledge that school would almost certainly be cancelled tomorrow, and in the likelihood that Dad and Bradford would be home from work as well.

The howling woke us all up around 3:00 a.m.

"Are you awake?" I whispered across the room to Marilyn.

"Yes," she answered.

"That wind is incredibly loud," I said. "Do you remember a blizzard like this any other time?"

"No," she answered, "not this loud anyway. It sounds like a wolf howling."

Mother and Dad were also awakened by the sound.

"Go back to sleep," Dad called to us. "We can't do anything about the noise."

The howling continued, louder and louder. It had a wild sound, filled with longing and a fierce and joyful triumph. I had never heard anything like it before and only once since, that occasion being one night when my husband and I were camping in Algonquin Provincial Park in Canada. On and on it went, wail after wail, crescendo and decrescendo overpowering the gale and filling the night with a strange and beautiful music.

"That sounds like a dog or a coyote," Mother said, "and it's somewhere close by."

"It must be the wind," Dad answered.

"No," Mother insisted, "it's a dog or a coyote."

"It's three o'clock in the morning. Who would leave a dog out in such a storm?"

"It sounds like Sam," Mother answered.

The dog that Dad swore wasn't a canine arrived at the front porch and scratched at the door to be let in. When no one responded to his request, he began to bark.

"Damn dog," Dad muttered, "I'm not getting out of bed to let him in. Let him bark."

"It's okay, girls. Pretend he's not our dog," Mother advised.

Sam began to sing again, a loud, beautiful, and sonorous howl.

"You'll have to let him in, or he'll have the whole neighborhood up," Mother said.

Unfortunately for Mother, who had already foretold the inevitable phone calls, the front porch lights of all the houses on our end of the street were already on, suggesting that the neighbors not only were awake, but they were also more than upset about being so. Two or three of them had ventured out of doors to identify the source of the racket.

I heard another expletive coming from the front bedroom. Although I had heard Dad use profane language now and then when he was extremely aggravated, those occasions were rare. He must be extremely upset, I thought to myself. He got out of bed, walked to the front room, and proceeded to turn on our own front porch light.

The telephone began to ring just as he was preparing to open the door.

"Hello," Dad answered the phone.

"One of your dogs is sitting on your front stoop barking and raising Cain," the voice at the other end of the line informed Dad.

As if we didn't already know.

"Yes," answered Dad. "We're just letting him in, and you shouldn't hear any more barking."

"This is a terrible night to leave a dog outside. Whatever possessed you?"

"We didn't exactly let..." Dad began to explain. The unidentified neighbor had already banged down the telephone.

"Get in here, you mangy flea-hound," Dad ordered.

Sam was not the least bit concerned over Dad's stern tone of voice or the dismay of the rest of us. He danced into the living room, snow-covered, and tail a-wag, seeming almost proud of himself. Wherever he had been and whatever he had done, he was a cold but jubilant dog. Marilyn and I let him into our room where he spent what was left of the night in peaceful slumber wrapped in a quilt at the foot of my bed.

The next morning several more people called to either inform or complain. The last of the informers was Esther Appleton who was very friendly to our family. Like a competent parish registrar, Esther recorded and regularly reported all of the neighborhood doings. She knew the name of every person in the neighborhood and where that person was and what that person was doing at any given time day or night, in blizzard or fair weather. What facts she missed were filled in with unique interpretations of what might have transpired. From two or three gardens away, one can easily remember and record what ought to have happened.

"Good morning, Mary," she greeted Mother.

Mother sighed. She knew she would be in for a long session answering Esther's questions regarding the previous evening's activities.

"What was going on at your place last night?" she asked. "I thought I heard a police car on your street. Lights were flashing everywhere! And the noise! And then I saw Thurston take off in the car. Did someone get sick?"

"No," Mother answered. "Sam got away from us and the other two dogs followed him. Thurston and Marilyn had to go look for them before they got into trouble or got hurt."

Mother was fairly certain that such a prosaic explanation would probably be embroidered in the retelling around the neighborhood. I think she was probably right, but we never did hear any more about it until spring.

Marilyn and I were out walking the dogs one afternoon when we saw one of my schoolmates with a plump black puppy.

"Want to see my new puppy?" he asked. "He's eight weeks old."

"Sure," we answered.

The puppy had a small white stripe on his chest, an otter-like tail, soft brown eyes, and a certain élan.

"He looks a lot like Sam did when he was a puppy," Marilyn mused.

I couldn't remember that far back, but I did see a remarkable retriever-like quality in the little fellow.

Over the next few days we noticed several other black puppies about the same age as the first. Even Mother and Dad began to notice a plethora of robust black puppies, some with a small white stripe on their chests.

Esther Appleton did more than notice.

"Mr. Fisher's hunting dog had a pretty large litter," Esther said to Mother and Dad when she came over for a visit and to share or collect some news, "and all the puppies look just like your Sam."

"Wasn't it about eighteen weeks ago during that terrible snow storm that he slipped out the back door?"

Mother cringed. Only Esther would take the time to calculate backwards to determine the paternity of a litter of puppies.

"Yes," Mother answered truthfully. "He came home later that night," she added. I think she was either feeling very defensive, or she was in total denial.

We really don't know for certain if Sam sired all those puppies, but the timing of their arrival and their remarkable likeness suggest that he probably did.

I'm thinking that Sam had a great night on the town during the first blizzard of that terrible winter.

Chapter 23
THE KENNEDY ASSASSINATION

I was in my last period vocal music class when the announcement came.

Unlike my primary school principal, who manufactured reasons to use the newly installed intercom in our building with pompous enthusiasm, Mr. Fairchild, my high school principal, was not enamored of anything or anyone that interrupted the instructional process. Of course, we had morning announcements every day during homeroom, followed by the Pledge of Allegiance and the Lord's Prayer. These were student led events, however, and were always preplanned. In fact, November 22nd, 1963, was the first time I had ever heard him interrupt classes to say anything. He was a rigid and humorless man, and even his infrequent visits to classes being taught by novice faculty were conducted in strict and uncomfortable silence.

"May I please have your attention!" he barked into the intercom.

"Students, your attention please. We have just received word from Dallas, Texas, that President Kennedy has been shot. I ask that we all pause for a moment of silent prayer."

For the next twenty minutes, the entire freshmen high school choir sat in stunned silence, awaiting instructions from our vocal music director. She too was immobilized as we waited further news.

Twenty minutes later, Mr. Fairchild once again interrupted our classes to announce, "President Kennedy has died. All students are immediately dismissed for the day and should proceed in an orderly fashion to collect necessary books, clothing, and assignments from their lockers."

We did proceed in a remarkably orderly fashion to our lockers. However, several of us called home prior to leaving school, which was required by many parents of that time whenever our schedules changed without prior notification. If we arrived either earlier or later than expected, our folks would worry that we had become ill or that something else had happened.

"I know," Mother said without preamble when she answered the telephone. She was amazingly brief.

"I'm on my way home," I told her.

I know now that the school officials waited at least an hour before announcing the dreadful news. They were waiting for final confirmation that the President was indeed dead and were also preparing the extensive fleet of school busses that served the four buildings in our community. Eventually, all the schools released us kids fifteen minutes early, but we were released in the usual order starting with the high school, followed by the middle school, and finally the two elementary schools.

When I walked into the house, much to my amazement, Dad was already there, and Bradford and Marilyn had been dismissed from work and were also on the way home. The television, which was never turned on during the day (Mother always said she had enough to do without watching the afternoon soap operas), was on with Mother and Dad both riveted to the updates. The newscasters were replaying Lyndon Johnson taking the oath of office with Jackie Kennedy standing beside him. Mrs. Kennedy was wearing a pink suit covered in blood and, although not crying or exhibiting any signs of hysteria, appeared to have aged a lifetime since the last time I had seen her televised.

"Air Force One has lifted off to return the body of former President Kennedy, Mrs. Kennedy, and President Johnson to Washington D.C.," intoned one of the announcers. "We will now take a short break and return to the air momentarily with continued coverage of this tragedy."

At that information, Mother arose to fix a quick "pick-up" supper. I began to set up television trays so we could continue to watch the events as they unfolded. We all knew that seeing a live broadcast dealing with the assassination of the leader of the free world was an unparalleled historical event. Nobody inside or outside our family could comprehend what had happened. We didn't know this drama was a portent of more terrible things.

"We have just received word that a Dallas police officer has been shot and killed in a neighborhood roughly three miles from Dealy Plaza where the President was assassinated."

Walter Cronkite was back on the air.

"We turn now to our sources in Dallas. What can you tell us about this latest incident? Is this related to the assassination?"

"We have no information yet regarding this, but as soon as we are informed, we will get back to you," answered the source.

The commentators talked on about what was happening in Hyannis Port where the President's family was preparing for the Thanksgiving holiday and what was happening in Washington, D.C., where Bobby Kennedy was awaiting the arrival of Air Force One and where Maud Shaw was caring for the two young children of John and Jackie Kennedy.

I was just about to get up from the little rocking chair in the living room when I heard the television again. "The name of the Dallas police officer who was shot and killed is Officer J.D. Tibbits. It now appears that the killing of Officer Tibbits is indeed related to the assassination of President Kennedy."

I sat back down and waited for more news. It was not long in coming.

"Lee Harvey Oswald has been arrested and taken into custody for questioning related to the murders of Officer Tibbits and President John Kennedy."

After this announcement, we ate hot dogs and beans from the television trays set up in the living room and listened to various newscasters filling airtime with information about what was happening in Washington, who would assume responsibility for planning the funeral, what was happening in the White House and in Hyannis Port, which dignitaries from around the world were preparing to leave for Washington D.C., and finally, when Air Force One arrive. At eleven o'clock or so, I left the television and went to bed.

The next day, November 23, it rained.

The focus of that day was the East Room of the White House where the President lay in state after the autopsy was completed. A Roman Catholic mass was held for the Kennedy family and some invited dignitaries, but most of the time the commentators filled the air time with snippets from the President's earlier life, or his time in office, or his naval service during World War II.

The weather was too wet for Marilyn and me to take the dogs for an extended walk, so we let them outside in the backyard for a short period of time. In between news broadcasts, I did what homework had been assigned, although we had received word that all schools were closed and that all non-essential workers were to remain home through Monday because now-President Johnson had declared Monday a National Day of Mourning. Monday was the day of the President's funeral.

The day dragged on. I can't remember if regular Saturday programming continued or not, but I do remember the constant rehashing of old news including the President's trip to Dallas, the scenes around Dealy Plaza, who saw what and where and when, and mostly many questions about why.

I went to bed that night wondering myself why anyone would kill the President even if he had political or personal differences. Such evil seemed up-close, personal, and warped, like a misshapen garment that had been laundered too many times and hung out in the sun to bleach and dry stiffly. I couldn't get myself around the awful fact of death.

Sunday the drums began.

The drums, the white horses pulling the caisson upon which the President's casket rested, the procession from the East Room of the White House to the Capitol, Chopin's "Funeral March," and the thousands of people lined up along the funeral route are my most vivid memories of the weekend John Kennedy was laid to rest. I also remember the scene of Jackie and Caroline kneeling in prayer at the catafalque and the members of the armed services standing guard around the casket. Then came the mourners by the hundreds and then the thousands, waiting in line patiently for ten or twelve hours to pay their final respects to the man, who in spite of his shortcomings, represented the future of the free world.

I can't speak for what anyone else was thinking or feeling that morning, but I was beginning to adjust to the reality that a tragic event affecting the entire world had occurred, and we all had to somehow pick ourselves up and continue on.

What happened next is a burn scar seared in my memory, an ugly and discolored gash that will remain forever.

"I need to check on the roast," Mother said.

She arose from the sofa where she and Dad normally sat to watch the evening news and their favorite television shows.

"And I'm going to let the dogs out," said Marilyn.

I honestly don't remember if I was alone in the living room or if some other family members were there. My impression is that I was totally alone at the moment when Jack Ruby, gun clearly visible in his hand, emerged from a crowd of people lining the way as detectives escorted Lee Harvey Oswald to a more secure facility.

On live TV, Jack Ruby shot Oswald at point-blank range.

A human vortex swirled into Jack Ruby and Lee Harvey Oswald, and within a few seconds, every reporter and cameraman was talking at once, trying to record and report what had just happened.

I was stunned. It was the first time I had ever seen anyone gun down another person so coldly.

I must have said something, for Mother and Dad arrived in the living room at the same time, and I told them what had happened.

"Some guy just shot Oswald," I said, "and everyone is milling around trying to figure out what happened."

The news people had more to report than they could manage, and the nation had as much horror as it could process as well. The world became an insane place. And for the rest of that day, television reports vacillated around foreign dignitaries arriving for the funeral, the huge number of mourners at the Capitol, reports updating the condition of Lee Harvey Oswald, the grieving family of Officer Tibbits, and new information about Jack Ruby.

Later that day, Lee Harvey Oswald died.

I don't think I was the only person who was totally numbed by this or the events of the day.

I was grateful for the respite of sleep when I went to bed that night.

The drums began again on Monday, the day of the funeral. Again I heard Chopin's "Funeral March" and saw the white horses pulling the caisson. I saw the Kennedy family with Jackie escorted by her two brothers-in-law, and the numerous dignitaries who had arrived to express their condolences. While all this was going on, I pondered what it meant to be a citizen of the greatest nation on earth. How would the death of our leader affect my own future and the futures of my friends? We had been told repeatedly in school that we were destined to be the leaders and salvation of the world and that we should conduct ourselves accordingly, responsively, and responsibly. I was certain that I wasn't up to all that. I wanted to be a kid again, to enjoy flying kites and riding bikes.

The drums and procession continued, along with the endless commentary. Every military unit present had its own specific place in the cortege; each played its own somber music, tragic and beautiful. I watched the caisson rolling toward Arlington National Cemetery and knew the finality of a young life ended.

I watched a little boy salute his father.

When Taps was played at the President's grave, I wept. I don't think I was alone; thousands of other viewers probably were doing the same.

By Monday evening we were emotionally spent from the horror, the high drama. I almost looked forward to going back to school for a couple of days before the Thanksgiving holiday set in.

But even school was not the same.

Coming so close upon the heels of the Cuban Missile Crisis, the assassination was already surrounded by rumors of conspiracies and unusual coincidences. My classmates, normally happy, typical teenagers, were subdued, abnormally attentive, and extremely serious.

And although we relaxed more and more as the year progressed, the assassination left us somehow different. We were a little more cynical, overly mature, and analytical. We were no longer innocent. We had changed. We had seen and experienced too much too soon.

As a generation, our birth into Post-Modernism, with its long, hard, and violent labor, had begun.

Chapter 24

SKUNKS

"We're off, kids," said Mother and Dad as they climbed into the station wagon Friday evening after loading up their camping gear.

Enthusiastic campers, Mother and Dad had been two of the primary leaders of the local chapter of the National Camping and Hiking Association or, as we soon began to call it, NCHA. Their leadership duties took them on weekend campouts all over northern Ohio and northwest Pennsylvania. On this particular late summer weekend, they were headed up to Cherokee State Park with their camping friends.

"The weather will be turning in another month or two," Dad said, "and we want to enjoy as many of these weekends as we can until the snow flies."

Bradford, Marilyn, and I opted to stay home. Bradford did not often join us for these camping experiences, and Marilyn increasingly stayed behind because of her commitments to local dog shows. Although I enjoyed spending the weekends tenting with my parents, on this particular occasion, I wanted to attend the first of my high school football games which was scheduled for that Saturday.

Little did any of us know what was in store for us as Mother and Dad waved good-bye and drove out the driveway.

Friday night passed uneventfully for all three of us. I reviewed my new high school class schedule eagerly anticipating the start of my new classes. I was especially excited about biology, a subject about which I was very keen, and about geometry, which I had heard was also very interesting. Bradford stayed inside planning an activity for the Boy Scout troop; he was an assistant leader.

Marilyn cleaned her new Nash Rambler station wagon and was loading crates in preparation for a Sunday dog show.

"Have you seen any skunks wandering around the neighborhood?" asked Mrs. Appleton when she wandered over to our back yard.

I figured wandering skunks were only an excuse for the neighbors to check on Marilyn, Bradford, and me. With our parents away, Mrs. Appleton took her neighboring duties very seriously and had already planned to provide Mother with a complete report on all our activities on Sunday evening.

"No," said Marilyn. "I haven't really seen any skunks around here."

"Well," said Mrs. Appleton, "you want to be careful. With your dogs outside so much, there's always a possibility one of them could get sprayed. You don't want that to happen, do you?"

"No," I thought to myself, "I certainly don't."

I could only imagine the brouhaha that would result if any of the shelties tangled with a skunk two days prior to a show.

Marilyn finished up her car, and I ironed my best shorts and blouse to wear to the football game. A heat wave was expected to infiltrate northern Ohio, and a long period of hot, sultry days was expected.

Saturday, as promised, dawned hot and bright. After a quick breakfast, Marilyn continued her preparations, which included bathing the dogs, loading all their equipment, and then checking to make sure nothing was left behind.

Meanwhile, the football game was as hot as promised. Although Claypool High School turned out division-winning basketball teams, and the golf and track teams were notably good, the football team was exceptionally uninspiring. Football had only existed as a varsity sport for one year, and though most of the student body either joined the team or attended the games, none of us knew that much about the game or how to play it. Over the next three years that situation was gradually rectified by the endless hard work of the coaching staff, some classroom instruction that focused on basic knowledge for the non-players, and the players themselves, who were enthusiastic and willing to try. Needless to say, on this particular Saturday afternoon, the football team did not set the world on fire with its prowess, and those of us in the stands were threatened by heat stroke by half time.

When I left the bleachers at the end of another loosing game, I was drenched with sweat and sporting a sunburn that promised to blister the next day. Nobody at that time worried too much about fostering melanomas, and a sunburn was the badge of a loyal and honorable fan.

"You're going to blister," Marilyn disapproved. Sometimes she was almost as good as Mother. She could pack an entire sermon into four words.

Bradford shook his head and wandered back to his room.

I sighed. As far as my siblings were concerned, loyal and honorable fandom shouldn't extend to blistering sunburns. Years later, I know that they were right, but at the time, the lack of support seemed harsh.

"Do you have everything ready for tomorrow? I can pack a lunch for you if you'd like." I tried artfully to dodge the criticism.

"Yes. I'm not going to pack a lunch. We'll buy something to eat from one of the vendors."

"That sounds good."

I was just as happy not having to pack a lunch. I went in to shower and change while Marilyn let all the dogs out.

I'm not certain how Sam once again escaped or why Shadow chose to follow him, but it happened.

"NO!" I heard Marilyn holler.

Then I saw the inevitable…a very determined retriever and an excited sheltie on a collision course with the largest skunk I had ever seen in my life.

A swift, nose-to-nose meeting with the dogs and the skunk turned and raised its tail.

"Oh, my!" I thought. "This is not going to end well."

Marilyn, fortunately, managed to dodge away from the tangled dog-skunk mass of fur. Shadow, with his swift and agile sheltie maneuvering, avoided most of the skunk's output. Sam, however, bull-headed as usual, took the full brunt of the skunk's defense squarely in the face.

He yelped as loudly as I ever heard him. I'm not sure if he was mad, angry, hurt, or mortally embarrassed. I do know that his cries could be heard all over the neighborhood.

Mrs. Easton rushed out her front door to see what was happening. When she saw the dog-skunk fight, she dashed into her house just as quickly and began shutting windows and doors.

Bradford, meanwhile, upon hearing Sam's cries of anguish, came to the front door. He opened it widely just as the skunk broke away and fled across Easton's front yard and into oblivion.

Sam, meanwhile, hearing Bradford's voice and sensing the door was open, made a grand dash through the door, past Bradford and into the living room where he dropped to the floor and rolled in agony on the carpet. He then jumped onto the sofa seeking additional relief. Finding none, he leaped from chair to chair, managing to leave skunk spray on every piece of furniture before tackling the drapes and then heading to Mother's and Dad's bedroom.

"What are you doing?" yelled Marilyn.

Bradford was stunned. The odor of skunk throughout the house was overwhelming. The only rooms Sam had missed were mine and Bradford's. Sam was in agony, Shadow was high on the spirit of adventure, Marilyn was livid with anger, and Bradford was abject with frustration even though it wasn't completely his fault since he didn't really know what was happening when he opened the front door.

I decided it was time for me to disappear into my bedroom.

Bradford, meanwhile, had managed to corral Sam and took him to the basement laundry tubs.

Marilyn filled the tubs with water and began to scrub while Bradford drove to the Claypool Village Market to buy a case of tomato juice. Several cans of tomato juice and a warm soap and water bath later, Sam smelled marginally better. I can't, however, say the same thing about the living room and Mother's and Dad's bedroom. The entire house reeked of unhappy skunk, but the two aforementioned rooms were by far the worst. We went to bed that night with all the windows and door wide open and a fan blowing through the house. The heat and humidity did nothing to alleviate the stench. I can't speak for either Bradford or Marilyn, but between the sunburn and the smell, I slept very fitfully.

The following day in the limited time available prior to Marilyn's departure to the dog show and Mother's and Dad's arrival at home, we tried to clean the living room carpet and upholstery as best we could. Marilyn thought hot water and vinegar might work, so we tried that, but I didn't notice any particular amelioration after we'd given everything two or three scrubbings.

"Stupid, stupid, stupid dog," Marilyn muttered. She continued to scrub.

"He shouldn't have been able to get out the door," Bradford mused. The fact that Bradford let him back inside the door was carefully avoided. "What are Mother and Dad going to say when they get home?"

I refrained from commenting.

In due time, our parents did arrive home, rested and relaxed from their short getaway. The weekend for them had been a success.

Mother entered the living room.

"What on earth is that smell?" she asked. "It's horrible!"

"Well," Marilyn began, "Sam tangled with a skunk."

"Oh my God!" Mother responded. "I can smell it a mile away, and how did he get back into the living room? And why do I smell pickles on top of the skunk odor?"

At that particular moment I decided the best place to be was on my bicycle riding into the sunset, kind of like the heroes did in Western movies. Only they rode horses, and I was no hero. I just wanted to escape the scene that I knew was going to follow.

"The smell is white vinegar that we used to try to get the smell out of the furniture and the carpet. He hit your room pretty badly, too."

Marilyn was determined to make a thorough confession even though she could hardly be blamed for what had happened.

"That damned dog," Mother said. She was half angry and half frustrated. But for once, she didn't blame Marilyn for the accident. She remembered that she too had moments when Sam had escaped from her very grasp and gone on one of his neighborhood jaunts. He had returned on that occasion only after rolling around in a meadow filled with cow patties.

The following Monday after Dad, Marilyn, and Bradford went to work, Mother and I had another go at trying to deodorize the master bedroom and the living room. Again, we were only marginally successful.

"Maybe we should hire professional carpet and upholstery cleaners to do this," I suggested. I was more than a little tentative, knowing Mother was particularly prone to confusing unsolicited advice with outright criticism.

"No," she said firmly, "that costs extra, and we can't afford it."

Some things are worth affording, I thought to myself, but I didn't say it out loud. I resigned myself to living with the odor as long as the warm weather lasted.

Two weeks later I started back to school. I was as enthusiastic about high school as I had been indifferent in middle school. Classes were exciting, activities were fun, and friendships continued to blossom.

Throughout that fall, I didn't invite a single friend over after school. The house had a miasma like no other in the neighborhood.

Even in December it had a definite odor of dill pickles, skunk, and wet dog.

Sam never did learn his lesson and continued to view all skunks as his sworn enemies. Only forceful restraint kept him from chasing down any stray skunks that he could see or smell.

Chapter 25
THE GREATEST GIFT

"Are you sure you want to go?" Mother asked.

"Yes, I'm absolutely certain. We've never spent more than one week in Summerfield since we've moved, and we haven't been back to the Cape since Grandma Harrington died," I said.

Adela and Angus had generously offered to include me in their annual family beach vacation on Cape Cod. After eleven years of longing, I was finally spending the first four glorious weeks after my high school graduation in Massachusetts–two weeks on the Cape with the McLeans, and two weeks in North Summerfield with the Thibidouxs. This time together was a graduation gift that both Grace and Adela had given to me. Knowing that it might be my only opportunity in many years to have such a holiday, I eagerly accepted their hospitality. After my trip out East, I would return to three major family events occurring back-to-back. The first would be Bradford's wedding in July, and the second would be Marilyn's wedding in September. The third event would occur a week after Marilyn's wedding; I was leaving for college. Mother's and Dad's nest would be empty by late September, but the four preceding months would be a whirlwind for the entire family.

Two weeks later Mother, Dad, and I were at Grace's and Louis's house.

"You're welcome to sleep in the dining room on the hide-a-bed," Grace said, "but you might be more comfortable sleeping on the porch."

"I haven't been on a sleeping porch since we moved," I said. "I think I'd like your front porch as a temporary bedroom."

"Don't they have sleeping porches in Ohio?" Louis asked.

"No. Ohio has too many mosquitoes in the summer, and our neighborhood doesn't have any porches, front or back, that are big enough to sleep on."

"What are your plans for the rest of your vacation?" Grace asked Mother and Dad.

"We'll spend only a little time here visiting and then take our time returning to Ohio. After all, we'll be seeing all of you in a month, and there's a great deal to do preparing for two weddings," Mother said.

Two days later they left, and my visit began in earnest.

"Do you want help with anything?" I asked Grace. We had just finished eating supper.

"You could help Michael and Steven get ready for bed while I give little Adela her evening feeding. I usually just fill the tub with warm water and Mr. Bubble and let them play with their toys. That way most of the dirt soaks off, and washing them is a lot easier."

Most of my babysitting throughout high school had consisted of either infants or older kids. Michael, who was four at the time, was the first preschooler for whom I had ever cared. Steven was two and likewise was the first toddler. I soon had the boys in their bath, and we had a grand time splashing water and playing with all the bath toys.

Grace had failed to mention the window directly over the tub wasn't any too secure in its frame.

I turned my back on the boys for maybe a second to lay out dry towels when a loud crash followed by a huge splash reverberated throughout the bathroom.

My heart stopped.

"Don't move!" I shouted. "Please, please, don't move!"

Miraculously, neither of the boys moved at all. In fact, they seemed generally unperturbed by a window coming down and landing in the middle of their bath.

"Don't worry about it," said Louis. He was standing with Grace; they had come to the door of the bathroom. "This happens all the time."

After my heart slowed to its regular pace, I fished both boys from the tub and managed to get them dried off and into their sleepwear.

I was thankful that I wasn't anyone's parent. I didn't think I could live through the experience.

The rest of my week with Grace and Louis was unforgettable. I remember quiet evenings watching the late show hosted by Johnny Carson, never imagining that seven years later I would meet and work for his first cousin at the University of Wyoming. I slept on the front porch of the house enjoying cool breezes on hot summer nights. We picnicked at Greenleaf Park; I watched countless episodes of Gumby and Pokey with Michael; I met many of Louis's cousins. Whenever they could, Grace and Adela took me to the places that I had loved and missed for the past decade.

We drove by the brown bungalow, now neatly sided and with an additional upstairs bedroom. We saw the elementary school that all of us had attended in turn, and we went to church both at St. Laurens, where the mass was occasionally celebrated in French, and the Methodist church which had been my home church prior to moving. Every visit for me produced moments of brilliant joy at reconnecting with the familiar and moments of sharp pain at the knowledge that these visits were only temporary and that I would not be returning for another half decade.

Two nights before leaving for Cape Cod, Adela came to collect me from Grace's home. She needed my help with some last minute chores, and she and Angus wanted an early start the next morning.

Once again I asked what I could do to help.

"Well," Angus said, "do you like to cut grass?"

Did I like to cut grass? Of course I did! Marilyn and I often vied for this most coveted of chores; sometimes we disintegrated into a squabble over whose turn it was to push the lawn mower over our acre of Ohio yard.

"Sure," I said.

"The lawnmower is in the shop," Angus said.

Interesting. I wondered what might follow this pronouncement.

"We have the old reel mower. It's hard to push," he said.

"I can try," I told him.

Within a couple of hours I was able to do a passable job on the front lawn with the old reel mower. Angus decided the back yard would keep for a couple of weeks until we got back from the Cape and he could pick up the electric mower.

The next morning, I learned that Angus was as much an expert at packing as Mother was. Unlike Mother, however, he had no illusions about the organizational skills of the rest of us, nor did he expect us to perform as a well-rehearsed drill team.

He packed the trunk of his large Buick by himself.

By prior arrangement, I was a passenger in Grandpa McLean's car. Grandpa McLean was Angus's father. Arriving from Edinburgh, Scotland, prior to World War II, he had built a successful printing business, fallen in love, married, and was devoted to Angus, Adela, and their (at the time) three children. He embraced Cape Cod like a native New Englander. He and his brothers, whom I referred to as Uncle Ian and Uncle Jesse out of respect, made most of the vacation arrangements, did all of the food preparation and clean-up, and provided regular diversions for the kids. Since his wife had died, Grandpa McLean had become closer than ever to Angus and his family, as had Uncle Ian, who was a bachelor. Uncle Jesse and his wife Philippa arrived in their own vehicle with young Jesse, their son, who was a little older than I.

We arrived at Beachside Cottages in Dennisport shortly after mid-day and, after unpacking, immediately went to the beach.

My joy was fierce enough to shred my heart. I was near the ocean I had always and would always love.

I remember countless happy hours swimming in Nantucket Sound, sunbathing on the beach, and walking to a little gift shop almost every morning after breakfast with Lynn. Even though she was not yet four years old, she kept up. Only occasionally did she need to be carried on my shoulders, and even then, she didn't need that much of a lift. I remember that Uncle Ian loved donuts, and we had them every morning with breakfast. By ten-thirty or eleven, we would be on the beach, there to remain until late afternoon. One day, when gusts of wind blew the tide into massive piles of spindrift and the rain darkened the beach, we went to the Woods

Hole Oceanographic Institute to view the large aquarium. Young Angus, aged six, was enraptured with the shark and whale exhibits, while Jean, at eight, enjoyed looking at the various types of fish and mollusks.

Halfway through this idyll, Uncle Dennis, who was Dad's oldest brother, and Aunt Marie, his wife, came to the beach for a day along with their daughter Jeanne and son-in-law John and their two grand-daughters…Jennifer, who was close to Jean's age, and Carolyn, who was a little younger. I had not seen Uncle Dennis and Aunt Marie for many years and appreciated the opportunity to reconnect with my extended family.

Shortly after their visit, Adela and I went for a row on the little tidal pond that lay between Beachside and the beach. That Adela actually did the rowing figures prominently into what happened three days later.

We had left the beach early that day for some reason that I cannot now remember. Uncle Ian was fixing spaghetti for supper and clearly didn't want help.

"I've matters well under control," he said. With his thick Scottish brogue, his boxes of pasta, and a concoction of spaghetti sauce, he made a colorful and unique chef.

"I'm going for a row on the pond," I informed my hosts. Adela was watching the three kids play on the swings and a small slide that lay in the middle of the circle of cottages. Angus was watching television with his father.

"Supper will probably be in an hour," Adela cautioned.

"Okay." I responded.

Proud of my newly acquired knowledge of rowboats and eager to try my skills, I set off for the small pond as the tide started out. Having observed Adela handily rowing us around the pond, I was confident I could manage just fine.

I was wrong.

As soon as I reached the middle of the pond, I began to row in ever-increasing circles, while the tidal current gently steered the boat toward the inlet that led to the ocean. I rowed harder in the hopes of redirecting the boat to its mooring point, but the faster I stroked, the bigger the circles became. The boat obstinately refused to go where I thought I was aiming, and the harder I tried, the more likely it seemed I would drift out to sea.

At that inauspicious moment, Adela appeared on the far shore with all three kids in tow.

"Supper's ready," she called.

"Coming," I answered.

Only I wasn't coming at all; I was going... farther and farther away.

Adela and the kids waited patiently for several minutes while I tried to maneuver the boat closer to shore. Then Angus appeared on the scene to find out what the hold-up was. Supper was ready to be served, and five members of the family had disappeared. When he saw me struggling with the boat, he, Adela, and the kids began to see the humor in my situation.

"Try using your left hand," Adela called.

"I'm trying," I said, "but the boat won't cooperate."

By this time the entire shore party had dissolved into laughter, and so had I. The situation was so ludicrous that I couldn't help it. At that point, I lost all control of the boat. Adela, meanwhile, had untied the second rowboat and came to fetch me. She attached a line and hauled me to shore, laughing all the while.

The rest of the vacation passed uneventfully. After we returned to Summerfield, I spent the final week with Grace and Louis before leaving for Ohio and Bradford's wedding. I had much time to explore and think, for this was the summer that I finally came to grips with the facts of my own life. I was finally back home in Massachusetts, but home wasn't quite the same. How I prized the sunset over the Berkshire Hills! I saw the Connecticut River singing its way to the sea with barges flickering red and green lights, and I had had two near-perfect weeks on Cape Cod. I could still smell the pine trees of Greenleaf Park, enjoy the laughter of family gatherings, but something was gone. That something was my childhood home.

That summer I recognized my memories for what they were: precious, tinged with longing and pain, but only memories. I was missing what I once had, not what was there now. Summerfield had changed some, but I had changed more. A part of me would always grieve the losses that had occurred when I left Massachusetts, but I had grown up. I had college and my life's work ahead of me.

Home…home…home…I let the word linger in my mouth like a sip of fine port…sweet and strong and filled with the flavor of grapes and the scent of apples. Home…my perfect summer, climaxed first by Bradford's wedding and then by Marilyn's.

As Angus drove Adela, the three kids, and me west to Ohio, I came away knowing that home, my home, was a place in my heart that no one could ever take away. I was and will always be forever a Yankee.

Many, many years later I was visiting with Lynn in her home, silently remembering the little girl that I used to occasionally carry on my shoulders to the gift shop in Dennisport.

We reminisced a little, but Lynn, who has my mother's love of music and my sister's sense of humor, could not remain serious for long.

"I don't remember much of that particular trip," Lynn said, "but I do remember seeing you rowing in circles on that little pond.

Chapter 26
BRADFORD'S WEDDING

Former President Eisenhower once said that before a battle started, plans were everything, but once the battle began, plans were useless. This adage could have applied to Bradford's and Lou's wedding rehearsal dinner. As the parents of the groom, Mother and Dad had the primary responsibility for this event.

The house had been dusted, vacuumed, and generally cleaned by the time the Massachusetts branch of the family and I arrived two days before Bradford's and Lou's wedding. Not only did Adela and Angus, Grace and Louis and their children come west for this event, but other relatives as well. Aunt Marie, Uncle Dennis, and Aunt Ellen augmented the numbers that would have challenged the most experienced and gracious hostess. Such a large and seemingly invasive crowd created untold anxiety and hyperactivity in Mother. She was in a tizzy trying to keep her organizational system intact and her guests in line. Having this event at a restaurant would probably have saved her a world of aggravation, but she and Dad would never have done such a thing. A restaurant meal that would have to include all of the out-of-town guests, Marilyn and her fiancé Edward, me, Lou's family, and the wedding party would have been a huge expense. Mother thought she could handle the whole crowd by having a buffet supper with the requisite cut glass punch bowl filled with a non-alcoholic beverage.

Mother's image of a sedate pre-wedding event where her guests and family could partake of a light buffet supper for their moderate pleasure and sober enjoyment was sorely compromised by the arrival of the New Bedford clan, especially Aunt Ellen.

"I just don't want anyone to make a bad impression on Lou's wedding party or her family," said Mother.

"What do you think is going to happen?" I asked. I was baffled that anyone couldn't like Aunt Ellen.

"Well..." Mother hesitated, "you know she likes to perform."

This was true. Aunt Ellen, one of Dad's older sisters, was more than a free spirit. She was a born actress and loved nothing better than to travel with an array of costumes in her suitcase. These outfits were supported by wigs, assorted props, some garish stage make-up, and a vast and thorough knowledge of many rag-time songs and dances. With all those items crammed into one suitcase, I was amazed that she had room for a change of normal clothing.

"I doubt that she'll do anything like that at a rehearsal dinner," I said.

"We'll see," Mother responded.

I felt sorry for Mother who wanted to present herself as the perfect hostess. In her heart she loved Aunt Ellen as much as the rest of us did, but her concerns had some legitimacy.

Lou was a quiet, gentle, and caring person, and Bradford had found a treasure when he met her. She was a registered nurse, and her soft, thoughtful manner of speaking was a sharp contrast to the Harrington family. We weren't exactly loud, but we were given to speaking our minds rather bluntly and were often tactless and insensitive.

The finger sandwiches were made; the punch bowl and supporting cups were assembled in the tiny dinette area. We had squeezed as many extra chairs into the living room as we could fit.

"I want to get in and out of the bathroom to clean-up and change before Marilyn and Bradford need to use it." I announced.

Our little ranch house had only one bathroom that we all shared. True to form, Mother had instituted a specific schedule for bathroom use based on our capacity for speed and normal usage of hot water. Normally my allotted time was right after Mother's and Dad's, and Marilyn and Bradford followed in turn. Of course, with such an unparalleled event as the only son's wedding, rules and schedules were suspended. Nonetheless, I didn't want to create a bathroom free-for-all by taking too long, so I bathed quickly and put on the dress I had selected for the event.

I don't remember when the rehearsal was actually scheduled or even much about the event itself. I do remember that the good Reverend Campbell, pastor of the Claypool Presbyterian Church, officiated–Lou and her family were all members of that church. And I do remember sitting in a pew watching the rehearsal and feeling extremely glad that Bradford had found someone with whom to share his life.

The entire entourage of thirty or more, including Lou's family, the wedding party, and the Massachusetts group returned to our house after the rehearsal. Everyone seemed to be enjoying the food, and we were finishing up our meal when Aunt Ellen disappeared for a few minutes.

When she returned, she was in full costume. And what a costume it was! She had on a very old purple and pink flowered dress that she had purchased from a thrift shop somewhere in New Bedford, a flea-bitten faux fur coat, mismatched pumps, torn nylon stockings with crooked seams up the back of the leg, and to top it off, a bright reddish/auburn wig topped by an ostrich feathered hat of non-descript color.

I heard Mother groan.

"I'm going to sing you a song," Aunt Ellen. "I'm going to play and sing "Second-Hand Rose.""

Sitting down at the piano, she began to play the familiar tune.

The guests appeared confused, but they looked on politely. Being entertained like this at a rehearsal dinner was beyond their realms of experience.

They hadn't seen anything yet.

After the initial rendition on the piano, Aunt Ellen got up from the piano stool and began to sing.

"Ellen," said Mother.

"I'm just a second-hand Rose," Aunt Ellen trilled. Her voice was very lusty in spite of her sixty-two years.

"Ellen!" said Mother. I recognized the frantic tone of voice.

As Aunt Ellen continued the song, she began to strip off her clothes.

I recognized that underneath her costume she had on the clothes she had worn to church earlier that evening. Apparently neither the guests nor Mother, however, did. Mother's face changed from faint pink to deepest red in color as more clothing came off.

Mother's flaming face was nothing, though, compared to those of her five children. Adela, who thought the entire performance a great joke, was laughing outright. Angus, who served as Bradford's best man, was more serious, but I could see the faintest hint of a smile lurking about his mouth. Grace and Louis, who had brought a gallon bottle of Pisano wine to lighten the mood and help the festivities along, both took large gulps from their glasses. Marilyn and I looked at each other, appreciative of the show but not really sure how to respond.

Bradford, however, was stunned into complete silence. This was not the rehearsal meal that he or Mother had imagined at all. I'm not really sure what he was thinking or feeling. He just sat there with a look of complete bafflement on his face.

I never felt sorrier for my brother or my mother than I did at that moment, but I had to admit that Aunt Ellen certainly had added something new, different, and exciting to what would otherwise have been a very staid event.

As she reached the end of her performance, she belted out, "I'm just a second-hand rose."

She pulled out her false teeth and tossed them into the air.

The performance was over.

The following evening the wedding was a beautiful candlelight event. I don't remember a great deal about it, though. What I do remember is seeing Aunt Ellen fling her false teeth through the air as she ended her show.

Chapter 27
MARILYN'S WEDDING

Mother finally had the wedding she wanted. Marilyn was the first of her daughters to marry in Claypool. Not only would Mother have significant input in planning the wedding, but she was also making Marilyn's wedding gown and my own attendant's dress.

Neither the McClean nor the Thibodoux clans were going to attend.

"We can't afford two trips to Ohio in the same summer," said Grace.

Adela added, "We don't want to pull any of the kids out of school that close to the beginning of the term."

Aunt Ellen loved a good party, and I was betting that she would come if asked, but she didn't have any means of transportation for a return trip since Aunt Marie and Uncle Dennis also decided not to return to Ohio that summer.

I noticed that Mother didn't press the New Bedford group all that hard.

Knowing that the extended family in Massachusetts was not coming diminished Mother's enthusiasm only slightly. She was finally going to have the perfect wedding, and nothing was going to interfere.

Edward Crosswhite, Marilyn's fiancé, was a fine person. Marilyn and he had met at the company Christmas party. Edward had grown up in the neighboring town of Elysburg and had completed his degree in mathematics at Ohio State University. Like Angus, Edward was a quiet, thoughtful person, and he was extraordinarily respectful of his own parents and Mother and Dad. He was the only one of Dad's sons-in-law to actually ask permission to marry one of Dad's daughters. I found this to be a charming gesture and incredibly romantic. The world around me, I thought, could do with more people like Edward. I liked him, and I was incredibly happy for Marilyn.

His Midwestern values dictated that before he and Marilyn married, he should provide a proper home. The house they selected, with help from his parents, was a quaint story and a half Cape Cod sitting on a rural road only a few miles north of where we lived. The house was just inside Claypool Township, another point in favor of the marriage. I didn't think I could bear to have another sister living as far away as Grace and Adela did.

"Wait until you see it," Marilyn said. "It's on Claypool Township Road and has five acres of land with it."

I could see the wheels in Marilyn's head turning. Five acres of land would provide her with all the space she needed for her menagerie. As soon as she and Edward had closed on the house, she took me to see it.

"It's perfect," I said. "I really like the whole place, but my favorite room is the big bedroom upstairs. It has the built-in bookcase and drawers, and the cedar-lined closet. The sloping roof makes it seem very cozy up there, and yet there really is so much room. And the oak hardwood floors are in such good condition."

I had to refrain from gushing; I was excited about their house.

Marilyn and Ed spent every spare minute of that summer putting their domicile in order. While Ed stripped and repainted all the kitchen cabinets, Marilyn cleaned and organized the large bedroom upstairs and then the two smaller bedrooms and the bathroom downstairs. They spent an entire anxious day deciding whether to lay carpeting in the living room or put down an area rug, and then they spent another day selecting furniture for the master bedroom and living room.

Mother, meanwhile, was extraordinarily busy putting the finishing touches on Marilyn's wedding dress...a beautiful satin affair with lots of beading. She also made my dress, for I was to be

Marilyn's maid of honor. Karen Dore, one of Marilyn's good friends affiliated with the dog show world, was the other attendant. Our dresses, appropriate for an early September wedding, were a pale yellow and mint green…Karen and I selected the same fabric and an easy, tailored pattern to sew, for Mother was making my dress, and Karen was sewing her own.

"You've done a fine job with these dresses," I told Mother after the final fitting. "Everything with the church and the flowers seems to be working out as well. Things are going very smoothly."

Even now, forty-nine years later, I'm willing to bet two-to-one odds that both Marilyn and Mother wished I'd have kept my mouth tightly shut.

Two days before the wedding, as Marilyn was returning from the mailbox with a fistful of letters, she slipped and stumbled over a small, unseen rock in the driveway. In an effort to save herself from falling, she came down very awkwardly on her foot.

"What did you do?" asked Mother as Marilyn, white with pain, came limping through the front door.

"I tripped over a stupid rock," Marilyn said. "I can't move my foot at all."

"Did you break it?" I asked. Her ankle was huge. "Do you need to go to the emergency room?"

"I don't know," she answered. For her not to deny immediately the seriousness of the accident was telling me a great deal. The pain was intense and the swelling significant.

"Put some ice on it," Mother commanded.

After a day and a half of treatment, the ice hadn't reduced the swelling at all and had eliminated the pain only minimally. The ankle was seriously sprained, and Marilyn couldn't bear to put any weight on it. A decision had to be made regarding how she was going to walk down the aisle on her wedding day. The use of a cane was seriously considered.

The morning of the wedding dawned softly and beautifully with bright sunshine, a cool breeze, and a beautiful serene autumn hint to the blue sky.

"The swelling is down some," Marilyn said. "I think I might be able to put a shoe on anyway."

Her new shoes didn't fit.

"I can wear sneakers," said Marilyn. "Nobody is going to be looking at my feet, and even if they did, nobody will see them because the dress is long."

Marilyn wearing sneakers to her wedding would have been perfectly appropriate in my mind. But Mother had other ideas.

"You aren't going to wear sneakers," said Mother. She was aghast at the very suggestion of such an impropriety. "It's your wedding day."

"Well, what else can I do?" asked Marilyn. "I can't wear the new white shoes I bought. I can't wear any pumps at all."

Mother thought. "I have an old pair of white ones that might work."

Her old, scuffed and dirty white pumps were at least one and a half sizes larger than what Marilyn, with her slender feet and perfect arches, normally wore. Mother's feet were wide with extraordinarily high arches and seriously large bunions on both of her big toes. Additionally, the shoes had formed strange bulges around the toe area where bunions had pushed out the leather. Mother's parents had never been wealthy and for many of her childhood years, Mother had worn hand-me-down shoes of varying sizes and styles. As a result, her feet were damaged almost beyond surgical repair.

"I can try them," said Marilyn.

One of Mother's shoes fit the swollen foot tolerably well, but the other one was too large. Marilyn's gait, while trying to walk in these strange shoes with mismatched feet, suggested something between an awkward lurch and a drunken stagger.

Mother's plans for a perfect wedding were skewed once again.

The hour drew near. As we arrived at the church, Marilyn's adrenalin kicked in. I suspect she was so thrilled to finally have the wedding take place that she was feeling nothing but happiness. Escorted by Dad, she walked down the aisle of the church in Mother's old, beat-up white shoes without a hint of a limp, lurch, or stagger. I don't know how she did it.

She looked beautiful.

Mother, misty-eyed and tearful as her third daughter was married, was also mightily relieved to have the ceremony concluded, the bride duly kissed, and the entire party moved to Fellowship Hall for the finger sandwiches, punch, and cake.

Marilyn had embraced her special day.

Mother had survived our childhoods and youth.

With Marilyn and Ed married, and Bradford and Lou settled after their own wedding six weeks earlier, I remained the only one of the five of us still, more or less, at home, and I would be leaving within the next ten days.

The week between the wedding and my departure for college was both the shortest and longest of my life. All of the shelties were going to live with Marilyn and Ed. The only animal that would be left was Sam. He would remain my special friend for another two years. Bradford's small room on the west side of the house became Mother's sewing and craft room. The house lacked the dynamic interplay of personalities that had been part of my life for eleven years. I can't say that I embraced the change.

As the saying goes, however, "Life is what happens while you're thinking about it."

As I packed away my childhood and youth, I came to the realization that I didn't necessarily need to have an understanding of life or of change or of the passage of time. Life, as messy as it is, is to live. I wanted to live life with something from each of my family members. I wanted to live life with some semblance of discipline like Grace, with the kind of knowledge that Bradford always seemed to possess, with joy like Adela, with passion like Marilyn, with sensitivity like my father, and with strength like my mother.

Each of them gave me so much. I am so very grateful to have had them in my life, to have cherished them, to have somehow remained closely connected to them in spite of a vast distance and age range.

I am so glad to have been born a Yankee.

About the Author

Mary Howland Harrington was born and spent her early childhood in Massachusetts. The youngest of five siblings, she grew up alternately in Massachusetts and Ohio.

This Book
Belongs To

Dianne Schmidt

CPSIA information can be obtained
at www.ICGtesting.com
Printed in the USA
FFOW01n0939100217
32282FF